The Mourners' Bench

How God saved an illiterate sinner like me

Aron "Paul" Seaborn

Bible quotations are taken from the King James Bible, Bible Pro mobile app.
Publishing and editorial support, design and production management by: Melanie Calloway
Cover design by: bookdesign/fiverr.com

For bulk purchase information, book signings, author's public appearances and speaking engagements, press releases or any other author/book inquiry, please contact Melanie Calloway:

M. Patrice Group LLC
704-280-8322
www.mpatricegroup.com

DISCLAIMER: The author has taken reasonable precautions to portray actual persons, living and deceased in an accurate manner based on memory, personal interactions and family oral history. Neither the author nor the publisher assumes responsibility for information that may be misconstrued by the reader.

ISBN: 978-0-9965190-0-7 paperback
         978-0-9965190-1-4 eBook

Table of Contents

Dedication

With all the hard work and time that I put into writing this book I would like to dedicate it to my children Zenas, Adrian, Kim; my goddaughter Denise; and the woman, who has been my backbone for years, my lovely wife Effie. Most of all, I dedicate this book to God who gave me the chance to read and write.

Acknowledgements

I would like to acknowledge and thank everyone who helped me along the way. Shortly before the passing of my first wife Martha, Grace McCaw and Mr. Mark Jennings took me under their wings and began teaching me to read and do math. I would like to thank my reading teacher Miss Lucy and everyone at Greater Homewood Adult Literacy and ESOL in Baltimore. I started my formal schooling at Greater Homewood. I went there for about two years. That is where I really started to learn to read. When I left Greater Homewood I was reading at a second grade level. I can't remember the names of the teachers at Sylvan Learning but I want to thank them anyway because it is all a part of my journey to read and write.

Many years later Miss Shirley Waddy continued to help me with my reading. While at Indian Land High School's Adult Learning Center Mr. Jerrod Funderburk and Kay Meadow were a big influence on me. They encouraged me with a gentle hand and they will remain a big inspiration in my life. At seventy two years old, I am fortunate to have three caring teachers at Lancaster Adult Learning Center; Greta Hough, Brenda Spivey and Patricia Threte.

I want to thank God for leading me to Liberty Hill Missionary Baptist Church where I met Pastor Michael Flowers and his lovely wife Angelita. I thank my whole church family because they supported me after I shared I couldn't read. They continue to pull for me and pray for me. They always give me an assignment to do during Black History Month. I have to research the topic which helps me as I learn.

I have special thanks to Sister Ethel Wilson who took time out of her busy life to teach me how to read the bible. Even though she is not living, I want her daughters to know she played a big part in my life. She was like a mother to me until she took sick and couldn't teach me anymore. I will always be grateful to God for placing her in my life.

I have a very special thanks to Carol Williams who saw me in school and took me under her wings for an hour and a half every week. She saw something in me that I didn't see in myself and I thank her for that. She is a wonderful, kind person. You don't find peoples like her today. I know God sent her to me and all I can say is, "Thank you God for such a fine person."

I also want to give extra special thanks to my wife Effie. She has been patient with me during this whole process. She encouraged me to write and share my story. She has joined me on this amazing journey. I thank God for Effie.

Most of all, I would like to thank the two wonderful people who was responsible for me being here now. They are deceased and looking down on me. They gave me everything they had and that was love and wisdom. I just want to say thank you mama and daddy, better known as Aron Seaborn Sr., and Minnie Seaborn. I love you.

Aron "Paul" Seaborn

Foreword

When we think about having the ability to read, some might disregard the fact that for many years in America, reading and writing was provided only to a select group of individuals who, by reason of lineage and fortune, had unlimited access to literacy resources. However, throughout the annals of history, other people existed whom had to uncover literacy's might through any means necessary. It was those communities, families, and individuals who knew the power of reading and stopped at nothing to attain it. They made sure that if there was just one book in the household, you would be able to read it. They knew being literate could take you places where illiteracy could not.

Consequently there was a growing population who, by no fault of their own, didn't know that being literate in America was the stepping stone to a brighter future and that the lack thereof was a detriment to this future. No, this group valued toil over textbooks and perhaps believed that a life spent working hard was nobler than a life spent otherwise. I believe we each can relate to one of the groups; maybe through personal interactions, but perhaps only through the person revealed in this book.

The more I reflected on this foreword, I concluded that my message should be to get you, the reader, ready for the impact of the life chronicled in this book and how that life indirectly impacts you. I believe that the best way to do that is by emphasizing the importance of literacy as well as the social implications that befall a culture without it.

The fundamental message in this book is about the most important obligation of an educated society—to prepare the next generation to be literate adults.

According to a study conducted in late April of 2012 by the U.S. Department of Education and the National Institute of Literacy, (32) million adults in the U.S. could not read. That is (14) percent of the population. (21) percent of adults in the U.S. read below a 5th grade level, and (19) percent of high school graduates could not read.

Aron Seaborn once fell into the fourteen percent of the populace that could not read. What is more disconcerting is that many others were not included in the statistical data that reflects our nation's ethos. There are countless men and women who, by the very nature of being born black and/or poor in America during post reconstruction, were never even counted. So because of the disparate trends of a racially divided nation in the late nineteenth and early twentieth century, scores of men and women existed without ever having the luxury of learning to read. Hence, many of their offspring suffered the same inequity.

Such was the life of Aron Seaborn. However, as he realized his own literacy deficiencies he vowed not to pass on this inexorable burden to his next generation. He did what was necessary, by any means necessary, to help educate his younger siblings and then his children, which disallowed his own involvement in academia. Insisting that he not be outdone by life, Aron now continues his walk toward literacy proficiency.

As we prepare the next generation of scholars, one of the areas through which we prepare them to learn is through "Literacy Forethought" which looks at assessments and benchmarks used for a unit of study prior to teaching the student. When done properly, teachers can change the lens through which reading and other subjects are taught because the focus is on the student and his or her individual performance. Less time is devoted to benchmarks that preclude the learning process, thereby rendering instruction more viable. "Literacy Forethought" can be the difference between effective teaching and disengaged students. When instruction is delivered with the end in mind, it allows for a clearer understanding of where the student must go. As educators, we can teach some of life's greatest lessons through this changed lens. We can instill cherished values, form endearing and enduring relationships, and experience some of our greatest successes through the students we instruct.

This is what literacy allows the student to do; to experience learning through engagement. When literacy is taught in a *proactive* environment versus a *reactive* one, we move away from assessments and shift our focus to the student and his or her outcomes.

Literacy forms the foundation of one's life or the foundation is not stable throughout that life. It can be the avenue through which people experience their greatest frustrations, their most painful losses, deepest humiliations, and most crushing failures. The lack of literacy can and will set up a person for a life filled with interruptions and staggering obstacles to overcome.

> *Literacy is not just the ability to read, write and speak. "It is the foundation upon which each of us builds our lives."*

In The Mourners' Bench, we meet a courageous Aron Seaborn, a man who utilized the knowledge he gained about life through the experiences he had as a farmhand, a successful businessperson, husband, father and black man. But through searing examples we also see the roadblocks he faced due to limited accessibility, inadequate opportunities and unwise decisions perhaps as a result of his illiteracy. Aron's childhood misbehavior might support the National Institute for Literacy's finding that 85% of juvenile offenders have problems reading. One would wonder whether Aron's poor choices and even still careless decisions as an adult kept him in the grips of illiteracy and the prison of despair. Perhaps it doesn't matter. What we do know is that Aron is one of many whom in the end, work with the hand they have been dealt. They continue to reach higher. By doing so, they set themselves free. Frederick Douglass wrote, "Once you learn to read, you will be forever free."

This is a book about freedom and the price we pay for those freedoms. It is also about the game of life through literacy and the absence thereof. How successful we are in life is often determined by both our freedoms and how well we play the game. How well we play the game is often determined by the quality of our foundation.

Those who read this book and take heed will uncover not only the blueprint for success, but the unwavering willpower and resolute determination to achieve it. Aron shows us that by having the courage to stand in the face of insurmountable odds, you can go after your dreams, you can achieve success and you can learn to read—at any age, under any circumstance. He shows us that it is never too late to fortify your foundation, whereby building up the vessel for which it supports. The liberation gained through reading supports and validates the power of literacy and its invaluable reach into the cultural mores of our society.

Rory T. Edwards
Educator

Introduction

Growing up wasn't easy for Aron Seaborn, the second oldest son of North Carolina Sharecroppers. Despite an intense desire to attend school, Aron was relegated to child servitude to help sustain his growing family. At the age of six, Aron had to forego reading, writing and arithmetic to plow a mule alongside his older brother and father in the menacing elements of the North Carolina summers and winters. He quickly learned that survival trumped studies. Subsequently, the lessons he learned as a child were a result of the harsh realities of segregated life in a small Northampton County Virginia township.

Aron longed for a better life, so he left home at the age of sixteen and headed for the big city. It was in Baltimore that he was given his first opportunity to apply what he had gleaned from years of working as a field hand. He was given a real job at a hospital by an unlikely sort of woman. Up until now, Aron's dealing with persons of a different race was unfavorable. By his own admission, "I hated white peoples" he confessed. But fate has a way of softening even the hardest of hearts. A kindly woman with white skin befriended him and gave him an opportunity which changed the course of his life, and ultimately, the way in which he viewed those of a race different than his own. With only a kindergarten education, he was given hope for a brighter future. In return he worked hard, if only to show his kind white benefactor that she had not made a mistake.

Thus began Aron's life of employment and his ascension from poverty. Hence began his love affair with money, clothes, women and trouble. His insatiable need to have more of each would take him down the unrelenting road of illegalities, deceptions and unmanaged anger. By the Grace of God and willful determination, Aron was liberated from the cruel realities that shaped his life as an illiterate, besieged and confused man. In the midst of unspeakable despair, he cried out from the depths of his careworn soul and found deliverance.

In the Mourners' Bench, Aron Seaborn allows us an intimate look into his journey fraught with hardships, successes, trials and ultimately—redemption. This is a survival guide of sorts; carefully bound into a compendious account of segregation, family life, agriculture, sociology, race relations, child labor, drugs, and the repentant life of a black man living in the United States. It is a bold lesson in courage and fortitude, hurt and forgiveness.

The Mourners' Bench should be required reading for students of all ages. In it, we are given an insightful glimpse into our own tussles with humanity. Truth be told, we all have a long way to go.

Like so many other avenues of self-reflection we have before us, Aron paints a selfless picture of imperfections. Lest we judge, we have all probably been confronted with biases and bigotries that we discount as part of who we are and how we were raised. Should we see ourselves through the prism of a conflicted nation, without looking within ourselves for our contributions to the whole?

As current events in our nation herald back to the days of Jim Crow and segregation, of modern day lynching's and police brutality, racial strife and discrimination, we must stand as change agents for a brighter future. No life should be deemed less than— every life matters. The Mourners' Bench is a timely reminder that we have yet a long way to go. I believe any time one allows an open window into their life, as Aron Seaborn extends through his writings, we can better relate to the unspoken attitudes that plague a nation…those deeply held beliefs and sentiments that lie in wait to be released in a barrage of unexpressed vitriol. Once a sinner— twice redeemed. We each contribute to the fabric of our nation; good, bad or indifferent. We are crying out for redemption once again!

I applaud Aron for taking a courageous leap into self-exploration and ultimately self-forgiveness. His willingness to share such intimate details of his life is not only admirable, but compelling. And while many individuals in the segregated south shared some of the same circumstances, Aron unapologetically reveal those unkind conditions in a way that causes one to root for his success despite the bad choices he made and the incredible odds stacked against him.

While Aron writes with a vernacular many will find difficult to understand, I hope others will see his words as a valiant attempt at healing—at finally being able to express a yearning that we all have; to be heard. Having done so, he implores each of us to perhaps take another look at our own discomfort with those areas of our lives we wish to keep buried. The book was edited for chronology and clarity of thought, keeping Aron's way with words, speech patterns and voice clearly his own, albeit sometimes contradictory. His past tense phrasing is inconsistent, yet indicative of yesteryear. His speech so powerfully illustrates that "you can take the man out of the country but you can't take the country out of the man." Aron is indeed a countryman, birthed to a nation yet divided, and still he is upholding his inalienable rights to live out the American dream.

Aron took a bold leap into healing the ills of a broken spirit when he admitted, as a middle-aged man, that he could not read. Now, Aron is running his own race. In so doing, he is fulfilling his fervent desire to learn; to be the student he did not have the opportunity to be while growing up.

We are all students on a path. Conversely, we are all one another's teachers. Let us stand for that which is right and just, allowing our lives to intersect with love and understanding. Carl Sagan wrote, "To read is to voyage through time." Aron has traversed time to excavate buried memories, emotions and experiences. In so doing he has become our teacher. The wise student will take heed and pay close attention to the lessons taught.

Melanie Calloway
June 2, 2015

BOOKS BY ARON SEABORN

The Mourners' Bench:
How God Saved an Illiterate Sinner Like Me
2015

My Struggle Through Life Was Worth It
2012

CHAPTER ONE
In The Beginning

The fear of the Lord is the beginning of knowledge:
but fools despise wisdom and instruction.
My son, hear the instruction of thy father,
and forsake not the law of thy mother.
Proverbs 1:7, 8

I remember like it was yesterday, mama calling for Peter and me to come in the house.

"Y'all come in now—come in and wash for supper!"

When mama call, we listen! There weren't no bargaining for something different. In those days, we play outside all day. But when it was time to come in the house, it was time to come in! Mama and daddy didn't expect to have to tell you something more than once! If they did, you could expect to get a whooping more than once!

We didn't have no video games or color television and such. No, our entertainment was what we find to do outside and who and what we find to do it with. We stay out playing all day without worry for nothing. I spent the first five years of my life playing outside and not much more. That is what we did back then. We didn't bother our parents inside the house too long. They tell us, "Go outside and play!" We went outside and played!

We lived in a red brick row house with faded green awnings over the windows in an area of Norfolk, VA called Liberty Park. There was a small front porch where we kept the mower. We had a tiny patch of lawn that daddy kept up.

One of my earliest memories of that front porch and that small patch of lawn was daddy telling us to never touch the lawn mower. We touched it once and by the grace of God I'm still here to tell you about it. When daddy told us not to do something, we sure better not do it!

When you walk in our house, you be facing a big framed picture of daddy on a flag hanging on the wall. Why mama wants to look at him on the wall when she come in the house is beyond me! Daddy wasn't an easy man. At least he wasn't an easy man when I was growing up. He let us know that he was the boss of his house and if you say different, then you go and be the boss of your own house! He wanted things his way and you better listen!

The living room was small. I suppose for a grown man, everything seem small when you think back. But when I was a boy, most things seem just right. How else it gonna be? It's what you have, it's what you know. For us, it had to be just right or it wasn't gonna be. We didn't complain. We couldn't complain. Mama and daddy did the best they could do. Everybody doing the best they can do. The living for this five year old boy was easy. I didn't have too many worries in Norfolk. I wish it could have stayed that way. I probably would have stayed in school.

There was a long green chair in the living room. We wasn't allowed to sit on it. Only company or grown folk. Just off the living room was the dining room with a long mahogany table and matching chairs. A mahogany china closet was across from it. A picture of a blond, blue-eyed Jesus hung on the wall above a long sideboard. I wonder sometimes if that be how Jesus really look. I suppose in the end it really don't matter.

We had good furniture when we lived in Norfolk. Furniture seemed to last longer back then. Maybe it was made better. Maybe it was because folks didn't let you sit on it. I think peoples took more pride in they work and in their homes. Maybe companies treated folk different then, I really don't know. Mama sold most of what we had when we moved to Enfield.

Back then, my Uncle Jack worked at the cotton gin in Seaboard. Sometimes, he bring home sacks of cotton. Mama use it to make seat pillows for the dining room chairs. Uncle Jack was mama's older brother. When he come to visit, they sit at that mahogany dining room table talking and laughing over a cup of coffee. Later on he come to live with us in North Carolina.

I could be standing in the kitchen right now it's so clear in my mind—small, with an old gas stove and a white, General Electric ice box. The floor was brown, dirty looking linoleum. That was the kind of floor that you could mop forever and it never look clean. Seem like some days me and Peter run in and out of the kitchen getting something to drink. Maybe that be why the floor stayed so dirty looking.

Mama used to straighten Lucille and Louise's hair in the kitchen. Fan in the window, hot comb on the burner, rag over mama's shoulder. Louise be screaming because mama burnt her ear or neck with the hot comb. My daddy wore his hair processed back then. Sometimes he get it pressed too. That's when some black men used to wear their hair long and straight or short and straight. Either way, it weren't nappy no more. Daddy's hair was so long peoples used to call him bird dog. A bird dog has long ears like a beagle. When he wore his hair long, that's what folks thought he looked like—a bird dog! He kept his hair like that 'til we moved out to the country. Then he got rid of it. He was a farmer now and no farmer could afford to keep his hair processed and long—too much dirt and dust.

It was fun living in Norfolk. We played outside all day most every day. If it be cold we play in the snow. If it rains we play on the porch. In the warm weather, the ice cream man pedal his cart down the street and yell, "Ice cream, Ice cream!" Children show up out of nowhere when they hear him holler. Sometimes there be fifty, sixty children with a nickel or dime balled up in their little fists, lined up to get ice cream.

Back then, there was no ice cream trucks or such; just a bicycle cart with an ice box on the front. The ice box was filled with a layer of saw dust on the bottom. A big ice block would sit on top of that. The saw dust kept the ice from melting. That's how the ice cream stayed cold and frozen. The ice cream man parked in the same spot under the same oak tree up the road. He be there the same time most every day. Soon as we hear the bell jingle and him scream, "Ice cream! Ice cream!" we run as fast as we can! We hurry home and get a nickel from mama so we can pay for it.

I didn't know how to read when I was five. I just point to the picture of the ice cream I wanted. I got the same ice cream all the time; either banana fudge or chocolate covered vanilla on a stick. They had an ice cream called a tootsie roll pop too. You had to push the ice cream through the cardboard to get it up to the top.

Even though I liked those, it was too much work just to eat it! I was one happy little boy licking on ice cream in the summer heat. Half of it would melt all over me. Mama would wipe me down and I go right back to playing outside. I smile when I see children playing outside today. You don't see that too often no more. We even played most of the day in Kindergarten. That was the only time I went to school most every day as a child.

Mama woke us up the same time every morning. She speak soft but firm. "Okay children, rise and shine!"

When she say it was time to get up, we got up! If we was nothing else, we listened to mama and daddy when they spoke. We know to listen to our parents when they tell us something or we get a whooping. Children nowadays have too much lip and not enough respect.

Peter and me shared one bedroom. We slept in the same bed. Peter is just a couple years older than me. My older twin sisters, Lucille and Louise, shared another bedroom with the baby girl, Minnie Mae. Daddy and mama shared the third bedroom. Sometimes me and Peter sneak into the girl's room and scare them.

We all take turns washing and dressing. I wore the same little shorts and button down flannel shirt every day. Mama look me up and down to make sure I put on everything the right way. I had a pair of brown brogan shoes that I wore to school and church only. Soon as I come in the house, off they go. We played outside with bare feet.

Most mornings we have a breakfast of oatmeal, cornflakes or rice. That was the only cereals back then. At least that's what we ate in our house. I didn't know nothing about Wheaties or any other cereals until much later in life.

If we don't have oatmeal or cornflakes we have fried mint grease. Mint grease was made with molasses and fatback. Mama take molasses and pour it into the hot fatback grease for about thirty seconds. That made the molasses real thin. Then she pours it into a plate and we sop our biscuits in it. We call it sopping—biscuits and molasses. It made for good eating when we didn't have nothing else!

In Norfolk, we always ate in the morning and we always ate at night. We always had money to pay the ice cream man. Daddy had a good job. I went to school. I suppose it was a good life.

Mama used to walk us to school with some of the other neighborhood children. You don't see too many children walking to school these days. Just a whole lot of school buses lined up. Maybe that is why so many children have health problems. I don't know. I just know me and most everybody else had to walk to school or we didn't get there at all.

The kindergarten school was in a warehouse-like building. Inside, the classes were sectioned off into different rooms. This is where me and the other black children went to class until we turn six. When you turn six it be time to go to regular school. I can remember brush painting most of the day. Nobody read in kindergarten in those days. Nowadays if you can't read by the time you get to kindergarten they think something is wrong with you.

We went outside for recess most every day. We played on the merry-go-round, the swings, and the slide. We run a lot too, playing tag or something. If we was not outside playing, we was inside brush painting or sleeping. I don't remember flash cards or letters on the black board. There was numbers from one to ten lined up on the wall. I don't remember the teacher reading to us. I only remember painting, playing, sleeping and having moon pies and milk for snack. To this day I still love moon pies. They don't make them like they used to.

After school the parents be lined up outside waiting for their little babies. There mama be with open arms. When I see her, I run straight into her arms. My mama was the prettiest, best hugging mama of all. And she was all mine for just a few minutes each day even if Minnie Mae was hanging on to her leg!

Mama didn't work. She was a housewife. She work hard enough keeping up with us children and daddy! Mama was a short and stocky dark-skinned woman who wore her hair pressed out and curled. She would straighten it with a hot comb and Royal Crown grease. I think every black person know what Royal Crown grease is. If your mama or daddy didn't use it, then somebody you know used it. Probably still do. She used to press Lucille and Louise's hair with the same stuff. Royal Crown used to come in a red, round cardboard tub. Now it's in a metal tub but it's still the same old grease inside. You could smell burnt hair and grease throughout the house on the days mama pressed her hair.

Mama wore either a buttoned-down housecoat or a shift. She wore the same old house coat. She had a lot of shifts in different colors. If she wasn't in the housecoat she was in one of her shifts. She didn't wear much else.

Mama always smelled good. She smell clean like Ivory soap and Jergens lotion mixed together. Mama always mix the Royal Crown grease and the Jergens lotion and use it on her skin. It made the lotion last longer. It grease dry, ashy skin and make her skin real soft. I still do it that way for my skin.

Mama always smiled. You never know if something was wrong because she always smiled. She was a sweet woman. Other people saw her the same way. If she had an attitude you wouldn't know it. The only time I can remember her not smiling was when she was upset with daddy. Even then she have a grin on her face like she know something you don't. She didn't like to see us upset over grown folk stuff.

Mama didn't drink or smoke unless she was with her sisters. That be the only time you see her with a Pall Mall cigarette between her lips. She be sipping on Schlitz malt liquor at the kitchen table with her sisters. I don't know if she was really smoking or if she was just trying to fit in. I can't even remember if she actually liked beer but I remember that big bottle of beer with the brown letters.

Daddy didn't drink or smoke neither but he always walk around with a twig in his hand like he was holding a cigarette. Daddy was always working. When he wasn't working he was doing something else. Daddy like to hang out on the corner with some of the other men in the neighborhood. They be down there just shucking and jiving. There was a big oak tree on that corner. If you stood under the tree when the wind was blowing you know it because the acorns fall from the tree and pluck you on the head. That oak tree must been about a hundred years old. I'm sure it heard a lot of stories and seen a lot of mess!

When the men is down there we like to see what they be doing. Some be drunk and cutting up cussing like the devil! Others be puffing on cigarettes or chewing and spitting tobacco. Most be sitting on top of wooden crates talking and singing, forgetting about the trouble of the day.

Sometime daddy call for me, Peter, and two other boys to come down where they be hanging. He line us in a row like we be famous quartet singers. We sing *Blessed Be the Name of the Lord*, and *Jesus on the Mainline*. They say I used to cry when I sang *Jesus on the Mainline*. Daddy tells me, "That's why I made you the leader! You got to feel a song like that!" I don't know if I always felt it, but I always cried.

We have spoons, sticks or something else in our hands pretending it's a microphone. Daddy set us up the way he want to see us and we shuffle around shy at first.

"Come on now," daddy say. "Show them what you can do!"

We would get to singing like we was in the church choir. We never rehearsed. We only sang those same two songs so we had a pretty good sense of how they was supposed to go. We had a time! The men sit there smiling, telling us how nice we sound! Peoples always said I had a pretty good singing voice but I don't know.

"Alright boys," they say. "You sound real sweet." Then they pat us on the head. As quickly as daddy call for us, he has us leave just as fast.

"Y'all get now. You done good." Sometimes we get a nickel for singing. Most times we walk away with nothing. I leave with tears in my eyes.

Daddy was something else. He didn't have many bad habits but he loved the ladies. Right up until he died he loved the ladies! Daddy used to say, "Anytime you see an old woman in my car, I'm either taking her to the hospital or I'm carrying her to the police." In other words, he liked young women.

Mama didn't like it, but she was from the old school. Women back then took a lot of stuff from their men. They did it for their own reasons. Mama believed in her wedding vows and I suppose it was gonna be until death they do part. But for daddy and his ways, she always say, "Time will bring anything in!" I didn't know what it meant back then but I know now. My mama was the type of woman as long as daddy came home to her at night, kept a roof over her head, bills paid, children cared for, what you do is your business. She figured, he grown—how could she break him. Mama knows, "All chickens come home to nest."

All in all, daddy was a man that liked to stay on the move. It was like he wasn't happy unless he was on the go. I don't remember him sitting still too long. Mama probably don't remember that neither.

Most weekends while we lived in Norfolk, daddy pack up the car and take the family to Seaboard, NC to visit mama's mother. Daddy come home from work around 6:00 on Friday. We grab a change of clothes and pile into daddy's old black Ford Model T. I remember there was two spare tires on the side of the fenders. Thank God we never had to use them. There were some dark, scary roads driving down Route 158. During those days, we don't want to be caught out on the roads at night. No telling what trouble find us.

The drive from Norfolk to Seaboard where Grandma live was about an hour and a half. The whole family travelled: daddy, mama, me, Peter, Lucille and Louise. They were the oldest. Minnie Mae was the baby girl. Sometimes mama would hold her. There wasn't no car seats for babies back then. Mama didn't pack no lunch or nothing else to eat. The drive wasn't that long. I either sleep most of the way or stare out the window daydreaming.

We pull up to Grandma's house and she come out and greet us with a smile and a big hug! She always had something for us to eat when we get in.

"Y'all come in and get cleaned up so you can eat" she tell us. Everybody go in except me and Peter. Me and Peter stay outside and play. We played outside in the same change of clothes for the whole weekend. Before we leave, Grandma wash the clothes on an old running board. She clean them with a chunk of Oxen soap that peoples in the neighborhood sold. If you don't have money they just give it to you. The Lord say to love your neighbor as thyself; the neighborhood was like family back then. Everybody looked out for everybody. It was easy to love.

Oxen soap was brown with a bad taste. Sometimes Peter, me and some of the neighborhood kids be outside playing and talking bad. Grandma hear us and yell out, "You keep talking that language I'm gonna wash your mouth out with oxen soap!" All she had to do was give us a warning. We knew that soap was nothing we want in our mouths! Oxen soap was some nasty tasting mess! If it get in your mouth you like to choke on it. And talk about sting! Today you have soap that gets in your eye it won't burn. If you have Oxen soap on your hands and happen to rub your eyes—watch out! Oxen soap get in your eyes and it feel like somebody sprinkled hot pepper on your eyeballs! It burn like the devil!

Grandma was always so glad to see us. She loved when all her grandchildren visited. Grandma had seven girls who all had children. Momma had eight; Aunt Alpha had seven; Aunt Teen, the baby girl, had three; Aunt Tiny had four; Aunt Mary had four; Aunt Addie had one boy; and Aunt Bea, the oldest, had three. Aunt Bea lived to be one hundred and one. We buried Aunt Bea in Norfolk, VA. in 2009.

Grandma's house was a lot of fun too. Grandma was a thin, dark-skinned short woman with a lot of fight in her. Even though she was little, if you did something she didn't like she would give you a piece of her mind! Nobody bother her and I mean nobody! She didn't like nobody messing with her grandchildren. If mama or daddy whooped us we would tell grandma and they would have to do some explaining.

"Now why did you have to whoop them like that?" she ask daddy. Mama didn't whoop us much. She always try to talk to us. But daddy—that's a story I'll share a little later.

Grandma wore her hair pinned up under a hairnet. I don't know if I ever saw her wear her hair no other way. Grandma dipped snuff. She pull out her bottom lip and dump snuff into it. I don't believe I ever saw her without a lump of snuff in her lip. She was a beautiful sight—hairnet on the head, buttoned-down house coat, and a big lump of snuff in her lip! That's how I remember her. Only a couple times she didn't have snuff in her lip. One was when she went to church. But you better believe as soon as church is over she dump that snuff right back under her bottom lip. Other time was when she died.

We loved Grandma's hot dogs and beans. After she open the can of beans she rinse out the can and use it to spit her snuff juice in. She kept one spit can in the bedroom and one in the kitchen.

She made hotdog and beans for us because they was my favorite! She serve it with saltine crackers or homemade buttermilk biscuits. All of us couldn't eat in the kitchen because it was too small. Grandma take newspaper and spread it out on the front porch. I don't know why we had to eat on the porch boards instead of the lawn furniture. She keep the lawn furniture on the porch. You know many years ago grown folk didn't let children sit on the furniture. No, you not gonna sit on the good living room sofa and chairs. Maybe she felt the same way about her lawn furniture. Don't matter though because her hot dogs and beans made everything right in the world! I could be sitting in the mud and I wouldn't know better as long as I was eating her hot dogs and beans!

Grandma's front porch run the whole length of the house. Long vines twined up wire on the front and sides of the porch. Big shiny green leaves grew all the way up to the gutters. In the winter the vines die back and in spring it come again. It grows so thick and high like a wall of leaves. I loved that front porch.

After grandma set us up on the porch for dinner, she bless the food. "Dear God, Bless this here food for the nourishment of my grandchildren's bodies..."

It was never a long prayer—short, simple and straight to the point. That's how grandma was. She taught us how to pray at night too. She told us, "Always say your prayers before you go to bed at night." She stand in the doorway while we kneel at the side of the bed and recite the Lord's Prayer.

"Our Father, who is in heaven..." I don't recall if I ever finished the whole prayer without stuttering through the prayer. I always say, "God knows my heart."

Grandma didn't have a bathroom in the house. She had a slop jar. A slop jar was about the size of large pot. It had a lid like a pot too. At night, whatever we had to do, whether it was number one or number two, we did it in this slop jar and put the lid on. Then when morning come, we take the slop jar to the outhouse, dump it, wash it out real good and get it ready for the next night. We lean the pot against the side of the house so it air out all day. We take it in at night. During the day we use the outhouse. Daddy make sure it's not too much brush growing up around the outhouse. Snakes like to hide in that. Grandma pour sulfur around the outhouse so the snakes don't come near it.

Everybody in the family was afraid of snakes except for me and Peter. When I farmed peanuts as a young boy, there be big black snakes under the peanut vines. They never bothered me so I didn't bother them back. I suppose they had more right to be there than me. It's normal for a snake to be in the fields. I don't believe it's normal for no six year old boy to be out there working.

Daddy loved Grandma. He always say she was our backbone. Back then I didn't know what that meant. If it wasn't for grandma doing some of the things she done for us, well, we might be doing pretty bad. She helped us out in a lot of ways, some even my memory don't recall. But daddy was crazy about grandma! I remember grandma cooking for us a lot, especially when we moved closer to her. Grandma had a special apron she wore most every day. She told daddy she want to be buried with her apron. When she died years later, daddy placed a freshly ironed and folded apron over her stiff body. That's the last time I saw that apron. That was the last time I saw grandma.

The weekend with grandma come and goes and it be time to head back to Norfolk. Daddy always fill up the car with regular gasoline before we leave Norfolk for Seaboard and then again before we leave Seaboard to head home. Daddy fill up the car with a dollar. Gasoline was six cents a gallon. That was real gasoline then. Today it is mixed with some of everything. I guess it still gets you where you want and need to go. Daddy step on that petal and he just drive, it seem happier than when he come.

Daddy gets to driving good and we either fall asleep or stare out the window. Me and Peter in the trunk compartment that raised up where we can sit. Lucille, Louise and Minnie Mae be in the middle seat, mama in the front with daddy driving. We travel from Seaboard back up Route 158 past nothing but solid woods and farmland: fields of cotton, peanuts, corn, soybeans, and cane molasses. Northampton and Halifax Counties was mostly rural farmland. There be nothing but farms and poor folk. I see men and women and children out there planting and gathering crops. Never in a million years did I think I be working in those same fields one day. Now when I travel down that same road, through those same counties, I think about my life out there. But now there are houses and businesses. There are still a few fields but I see people and cars, restaurants and gas stations. Probably still plenty of poor folk too.

Sometimes mama and daddy take us to Aunt Mary's house in Norfolk on a Sunday. We hardly went to church on Sunday. Sometimes we travel after church but Sunday was our day to go to visit folk. If we wasn't in Seaboard visiting grandma we be at Aunt Mary's. She and Uncle Louis live about four blocks from us. Aunt Mary and Uncle Louis had three girls and one boy. Louis Jr. was around the same age as me. He was my favorite cousin. Louis had a bicycle. We go across the street to the park most times. Me and Peter take turns trying to ride his bike. We didn't know how to ride a bike. We never had one. I used to tell myself that when I got grown there is four things I'm gonna have; money, cars, clothes and a bike. I said I'm gonna have me a bike and I do! In other words, put in your mind the things you want. Work and pray, and watch it happen. I've had a bike ever since I bought my first one. Buying my first bike was like kissing a girl for the first time—sweet! Me and my second wife Effie ride our bikes throughout our neighborhood to this day.

Louis let us ride his bike most of the time. We fall down and tear up our clothes a lot. By the time we get back to the house we be so dirty with knees all skinned up. But those were happy days. I loved my little life in Norfolk.

Some Sundays we go to Aunt Tiny and Uncle Boot's house. His name was Boot Long. That's all I ever knew. If he had another name I don't know about it. They lived about six miles away so we all pile into the Model T and make our way down the road. Aunt Tiny had three boys and one girl. They had bicycles too. I loved going to their house. When mama and daddy say, "let's go", we was ready! We loved riding their bikes. That's how I learned how to ride; by riding my cousin's bikes.

Most of my cousins did pretty well in life. Louis Jr. has passed away. God has called him on to Glory. But to this day I still visit his sisters. I see pictures of Louis from back in the day when he was a young man. We had some good times together. He taught me how to ride a bike. I taught him how to ride a mule and a horse.

Daddy was a hard worker. He always worked and took care of his family. He was employed by Old Bay Line Trucking Company. I know that like it was yesterday. I remember him driving the green paneled, open back truck home and pulling up to the curb. He carried things that they used to make record players with. He take the goods around to different companies that sold record players. He didn't sell them but he was the truck driver that delivered them.

I remember him taking some of the goods, selling it on his own to peoples around town. After a while he got caught. He went to jail for three days for stealing. Somebody called Uncle Louis. Uncle Louis is who got him the job. Uncle Louis knew everybody in Norfolk. I always thought he was like the mayor. I think he was a mason too. He was a big deal. At least to a small boy he seemed like he was a big shot. He had his own business. I never knew what he did in his business but he got daddy's charges dropped. He got my daddy out of jail. Maybe that's where I got my business sense. I don't know. But Uncle Louis went to vouch for him and Old Bay Line didn't press charges. As of this writing Uncle Louis is still single living in Norfolk. He never remarried after Aunt Mary passed away.

We were living well when we were in Norfolk. We weren't on a farm slaving for the white man. Everybody we knew was living well. We had everything we needed. As a little boy I thought we was rich. Can you imagine? I don't ever remember being without something we needed. A lot of folk would call that rich.

We played outside a lot finding something to keep us busy. We roller-skated a lot. We skate up and down the street half the day. The skates then were the old-time metal ones with four wooden wheels. The shoe of the skate slid back and forth to fit your foot. You need a wrench to tighten them. We used to play whiplash on our skates. Everybody hold hands and swing around real hard. If the end person isn't holding on tight he's going down! The line would snap like a whip! That's why it was called whiplash. That was one of our favorite games.

We also rode our scooters on the sidewalks and in the streets. One time, Peter was coming down the street on his scooter going one way and I was coming down fast from the other side. There was a car parked in between us and we didn't see each other. We crashed into each other so hard that one of my front teeth got knocked out! We just got up, ran to the house where mama wiped us down and brushed us off. Twenty minutes later we back out doing the same thing over again!

Another time, I was out playing cowboy. All the kids be playing, talking and laughing. I was a stutterer. Some of the kids like to tease me and laugh at me. I didn't like that. It didn't matter if it was a boy or girl—I'd jump on them and start fighting. I fought like I was a cowboy in the Wild West. I was always fighting over something! Sometime it was an innocent tussle; other times it be a real good scrap! The neighbor come to the door or come outside yelling, "What's going on?" grabbing us by the collar, pulling us to come with her. "If you can't play together nice then go home!" I go home crying and mama ask, "What's wrong with you boy?"

"They was teasing me because I was stuttering." It took a long time to get those words out of my mouth. Crying and stuttering don't mix too good when you got something to say.

"Well boy, fighting ain't gonna solve nothing. Don't you know you catch more flies with honey?" I didn't know that.

Mama know I have a temper. I don't know where it come from but I was quick to fight. I'm not proud of all the fights I had. Many times I should have walked away but when you young you don't know no better. Some of the fights I started, some I was just standing up for myself. Daddy taught us to always stand up for ourselves. Today I hold my tongue. I'm not so quick to anger. I suppose some of that is because I'm older, some is because of what mama taught me, but most is God's Grace.

If I start a fight, I either have to stay in the house while all the other kids still playing outside or I have to stay in the yard by myself. By the next day we all be playing together again like nothing ever happen!

Me and Peter be running and horsing around all the time, getting into stuff we shouldn't be doing. One day Peter decides to take the lawn mower off the front porch and run it over the lawn. This was the black push mower with the rotating blades that daddy told us to never touch! But we decides we gonna be big and cut the grass. My baby sister Minnie fed some paper into the lawn mower as we was pushing it back and forth. Minnie happened to push the paper down too far and we chopped two of her little fingers right off! She let out a scream that sent chills down my spine. We knew we was in for it. She screamed, we screamed and didn't know what to do. Mama come to the door.

"What's all that screaming for?"

We couldn't say a word. We stood there frozen in fear because we know we wasn't supposed to be playing with that lawn mower. And poor little Minnie Mae was standing there with blood dripping all over her from her hand! When mama saw Minnie, a panic set in on her face that I never seen before. She picked Minnie up and ran to the neighbor. The neighbor found the two fingers, wrapped them in a towel and rushed mama and Minnie to the hospital. We was hoping they be able to sew them back on her hand but they couldn't. All the doctors did was bandage up the fingers that was left and send her on her way. That is how it remains to this day. Minnie has a hand with only three fingers.

When we got home from the hospital we knows what was coming. Mama didn't do nothing to us but daddy gave us a whooping so bad I'll never forget it! When he come home from work that day and he saw Minnie's hand he asked mama, "What happened to her?" Mama told him what we did. He walked toward us while he was taking off his belt.

"Now didn't I tell you not to touch that lawn mower unless I was present?"

"Yes daddy" I said, shivering in my pants. I knew I was about to get a real good whooping.

Daddy used to wear a thick leather belt. Years ago it was a better grade of leather. When he pull it off I knew what was coming. Daddy don't pull his belt off for nothing.

"You think you got away with something before" daddy says. "Now I'm gonna give it to you old and new!"

He ran his hand down that fat leather belt and whooped Peter first. He whooped me next. Then he went from me to Peter and back again from Peter to me. After what seem like an hour of whooping mama asked, "Now Earl, don't you think that's enough?" Daddy pushed her aside and kept whooping us until he was satisfied. That whooping felt like he was strapping down on us forever! Might be the worst whooping I ever got. I don't know if a five year old child ever need to get beat that bad no matter what they done.

After daddy beat us long and hard he told us, "Whatever work Minnie Mae has to do, as long as you under my roof you will do it for her! Don't you forget that!"

Mama bathed us that night and put salve all over us. I could feel the soothing of that salve but it wasn't enough to take away the pain. Mama had a gentle way about her so most times it softened daddy's hard edge. But no softness in the world was gonna take away the sting of that whooping. Going to school the next day with a mark on you—and I had plenty of them—didn't matter. There was no such thing as child abuse back then. Parents could whoop their kids all day and nobody thought nothing of it. Matter of fact, the teachers could whoop you, the neighbors could whoop you, your aunts and uncles could whoop you—that's just how it was! We never touched that lawn mower again unless daddy was around and he gave us permission to touch it!

That wasn't the only whooping we ever got. We got plenty. I seem to get more than everybody else because I was always fighting and getting into trouble. I remember one time I did something daddy didn't like. The older ones was responsible for the younger ones so if one did something wrong, everybody had to suffer. He lined all of us up and whooped us going down the line. After he finish whooping us he say to us, "now tell daddy thanks for what I done to you". He don't want to hear no sniffles. If you sniffle while you tell him thanks, you get a few more licks. He go to the first one in line and tell them to thank him without sniffling. By the time he got to the end of the line where I was standing, I won't be sniffling. I say, "Thank you daddy for what you done to me."

My father's firm hand made me the man I am. I can't say whether he was right or wrong for doing what he done. I believe he done the best he know how to do. To this day I don't hold nothing against my daddy for doing that. I really do thank him.

CHAPTER TWO
Honor Thy Father and Mother

My son, hear the instruction of thy father,
and forsake not the law of thy mother:
for they shall be an ornament of grace upon thy head,
and chains about thy neck.
Proverbs 1:8-9

We moved from Norfolk to Enfield, NC during the summer after I turned six. It was a hot North Carolina summer and school was about to start in a few weeks. Daddy lost his job with Old Bay Trucking and mama wanted to be closer to her family. A job was hard to come by and nobody hire daddy. I remember mama saying, "Thank God Paul don't have to stay home another year." She was talking about me being able to go to school with the girls. If you weren't six before the start of the school year you wait a whole school term before you start. I was happy I turned six so now I can ride the bus to school with the girls. I could go to school and learn the alphabet and words. I was gonna learn how to count and add. I thought this was the start of a better life than what I knew in Norfolk. And if you had asked me, I thought my life in Norfolk was pretty good!

We got to Enfield and a few weeks later when school started, I knew I wasn't going. I don't know if daddy ever told us that we wasn't going to school and that we was gonna have to help on the farm all day. All I know is the last part of my first summer in Enfield was spent with Daddy in the field preparing the land for the fall crops. I didn't know nothing about sharecropping, about tilling the land, plowing a mule or nothing else. I didn't know that this was gonna be what I had to do every day. But I found out soon.

There was a farm available that we could work on and that's how we end up in Enfield after daddy lost his job in Norfolk. We moved into an old grey clapboard-sided house about half mile off the main road. You couldn't see it from the street. We had to climb over a red clay hill to get to the house. It wasn't like our house in Norfolk. It seemed smaller, darker, worn. There was holes and cracks in the windows. The floorboards had large cracks in them too. It wasn't much but it was what we had.

Mr. Quincy, another black sharecropper, lived behind us. Mr. Quincy was a short, dark-skinned man who loved to dip his snuff. I see him coming down the road with his mule and wagon. He didn't have a car so he used his mule and wagon to go to town with Miss Victoria and his girls. They used to take the dining chairs out the kitchen and set them in the wagon. That's how they travelled to town to get their groceries and supplies. They light the lanterns on the side of the wagon so people can see them on the road when dusk fall.

Mr. Quincy loved his juice once and awhile. If the family didn't go with him, he go alone and stop for a couple drinks of liquor. Sometimes he have too much but the mules knew how to get home. They turn right in to the roads that lead to his house. By the time the mules get up to our house, we see Mr. Quincy laying in the wagon knocked out! Sometimes me and Peter would lead the mules to his house. Miss Victoria say, "Just leave him in the wagon. He be alright." So we leave him there and walk home.

Mr. Quincy was a little bit older than daddy. He was a nice man. He and Miss Victoria had two sons, Johnny and Joe and two girls, Erma and Louise. Both Johnny and Joe didn't go to school either. They had to help Mr. Quincy on the farm. They sharecropped on Mr. Fleetwood's farm like us. There was no other houses on the farm. There was a white family across the field. I never even really paid attention to black and white before I moved to Enfield. In Norfolk, almost everyone around us was black so that is what I knew. Here, seem like all the black folk was on a white man's farm. It was hard not to notice that.

The man that lived across the field with his wife was a mean old white man! I don't know if I ever learned his name. He lived there with his wife. Don't know that I ever learned her name either. They didn't speak to us. They never waved when they saw us. They barely saw us it seemed, even though they be looking right at us! He might not like black folk. It's just how it was back then. I didn't really think much about it. Matter of fact, I think he was so mean because he knew me and Peter had an eye on his fruit.

They had apple, pear and peach trees on the property around their house. It reminded me of an orchard. That man, he had some beautiful fruit. I always wanted to taste the fruit out of that white man's orchard. I wanted it bad!

One day me and Peter watch the house and wait for them to leave and go to town. School had started, the air was cool, the apples and pears was ripe for the taking! We run down to his yard and picked the apples and pears off the ground under the trees. They was some of the biggest, prettiest apples and pears I ever seen. I thought we couldn't be doing too much harm because we picking them off the ground. Then we went over to the peach tree. There wasn't much on the tree; the season for peaches come and gone. Peter climbed the tree anyway. He thought he was grabbing a peach. Instead he grabbed a big ole yellow jacket nest! He fell out the tree just a screaming and hollering! The yellow jackets come out the tree buzzing behind him. It was a big swarm. They buzzed their way straight to his head! Peter was trying his best to fight them bees off of him. But those bees got right on the top of his head and got the best of him. His arms was swinging every which way. He managed to knock off most of them. I was screaming and running right behind him trying to catch up. I wanted to help him but by the time I caught up most of the bees had either stung him, been swatted dead or they flew away.

We got home and mama washed his head with witch hazel. She made a paste out of alcohol, liniment and snuff and rubbed it in the spot and got the stingers out. Then she washed his head with Epsom salts to get the swelling down. It was a while before the swelling went down. Before long the area on the top of his head where the bees stung him started turning red and thin. It took a few months for his hair to grow in. As Peter got older, his hair just stopped growing in that spot. He never grew hair there again. We got the fruit, Peter got a bald head and we both got a whooping too. I tell you we never went back to that white man's yard!

Anytime we had a scrape or cut mama always clean the spot and put her magic paste on it. Fifteen minutes after she put that paste on the sore you never know something was there. I was playing around with the hatchet one day and split the skin under my thumb wide open! Mama cleaned it out the same way; alcohol, liniment and snuff. Then she wrapped my thumb with cheese cloth. To this day I only have a small scar. It might flame out once and a while but it don't usually bother me. Another time me and Peter was running around outside. I stumped my big toe so bad that the skin was left hanging off. Mama treated it the same way and wrapped the toe in cheesecloth. It was good as new in a few days. We couldn't go to the doctor. We lived too far out. No, there was no doctor for us. The only way you see a doctor is if you got carried to the hospital for something really serious. We was a long way from the hospital. Mama was our doctor.

I loved fruit. Some Saturdays I yell out, "Mama, we going huckleberry hunting!" We get up and go hunting for berries: me, Peter, Lucille, Louise, Minnie Mae. Berry season don't last too long. They grow wild in the woods—huckleberries, blackberries. Sometimes we be out in the woods walking miles, sniffing and smelling. We break twigs and sticks so we can find our way back home. Me and Peter scare the girls while we in the woods. We throw something when they're not looking and yell, "There go the boogey man!" Louise and Lucille go screaming and running!

There wasn't no wearing shoes; we be barefoot, stepping on prickly briars. If you miss your footing and step on a briar the needles get stuck deep in your feet like splinters. Sometimes we pull them out and go our way. Other times you might not know a needle was in there until a few days later when your foot swell up and start to hurt. When that happen, mama get a piece of fat back and take cheese cloth, tie it to your feet and cover it with a sock. The next morning, the splinter be right at the top of your skin and mama pull it right out. I loved mama.

We could tell when we getting close to the huckleberries because we smell the sugar just floating in the air. When the smell be real strong, we stop, and it be right there—a patch of huckleberries as big as a football field! We pick and eat and pick and eat. Our hands be stained purplish-blue by the time we finish. Sometimes I tease the girls by saying, "If you don't give me your huckleberries I'm gonna leave you!" Of course we won't ever leave them.

Me and Peter take turns carrying Minnie Mae through the woods. She was too little to walk barefoot the whole way. But we get home happy with sacks and bucket loads of huckleberries. By the time we get home the sack be blue from the huckleberry juice. The white peoples come from town just to buy our berries. We sold them for a quarter a pint or fifty cents a quart. We made a little money selling those berries. All of us got to keep the little bit of change we got.

When Peter and me drive the mules and wagon to town and take cotton to the gin, on the way home we stop at the store and buy candy with our change. The girls couldn't go to town with us so they tell us what they want.

"I want orange and grape soda or Pepsi or RC cola," Louise say. Sometime she can't make up her mind!

Lucille yell, "Get MaryJanes too!"

Me and Peter got jawbone breakers, sugar daddies, sugar babies and BB bats. We carry those in our pockets while we work in the fields. We also got the strawberry, chocolate and vanilla ice cream. We loved ice cream. We didn't know it had a name. And that didn't matter anyway because we didn't know how to read. We just knew that the three flavors of ice cream come together. It was a treat for us to be able to buy those few things with money we earned ourselves. So in a sense, I been working since I was six years old.

It didn't matter if we could read no how because we couldn't go in the store and pick up nothing. In the Jim Crow south a black person wasn't allowed to shop and walk through the store. You go in the store up to the counter and you either tell the man what you want or hand him a note and he get it for you. Strange enough, I couldn't read but I knew a nickel from a dime. If I paid for something that costs a nickel and I gave the man a dime, I know

I was supposed to get a nickel back. I knew about numbers and money even at that age.

In kindergarten big sheets of colored construction paper with numbers written on them was tacked to the wall. We didn't learn about letters but we learned our numbers. I know it must have been the grown folk way of preparing us to not be cheated out of our money. Years later my little sister Minnie Mae come home from school and teach me math. I never understood how Minnie Mae started school after me and she was able to pass me and teach me things. I could never understand that. I didn't realize then that I had to go to school all the time to keep up with the lessons. And I had to keep up with the lessons to be promoted to the next level. But I kept up with the number lessons she taught me. I suppose those few lessons stayed with me because I was always good with numbers, even when I couldn't read or write.

Growing up poor in the south we found things to do with our time. If we wasn't berry picking or playing cowboys and Indians, we go clay dirt hunting. We find a big steep hill and dig until we get down about six inches. We know when we hit it because when you hit the right spot it is real soft. You talk about something good! We scoop out the clay and roll it up it our hand to the size of a big orange. Then bite into it and oh my goodness, it was so sweet we could have been eating candy! Yes, it was caramel clay, that's what it tastes like. Mama give us a spoonful of castor oil because we get bound up after eating all that clay!

Sometimes we be playing or working so hard all day we go to bed without ever washing up. We just too tired! Wherever we lay at night, that's where we sleep. Then morning come and if we don't wake up from the rooster crowing and the cows mooing then mama wake us up. And like I said if mama say to get up, then we get up! There ain't no begging if we can stay in bed another five minutes. We didn't pull the covers over our heads and stay put. No, we got our butts up!

We didn't have a tub so we use the wash pan. We pour hot water from the kettle on the stove into the pan. The wash pan was used for a quick clean up. Whoever used the pan first wash up and dump the water out, and then the next person fill it up and do the same. The last person that uses it has to clean and hang it on the nail on the screened-in porch. That's where we hang all the wash pans. We had a few.

Mama also had big foot tub that she sit on the wood stove. Me and Peter had to chop wood in foot lengths and cut them into smaller pieces to feed into the stove. Mama fill the foot tub with pails of water from the well. We used that when we needed to wash our whole bodies; face, neck, underarms, private parts. This wasn't no real bath in a bath tub. We carry a big wash pan to the bedroom and wash up the best we could and be done. I can't remember having an actual bath when I was a boy. Not where you sit in a tub of water and soak for a long time like people do today. And the only shower we had was if we stood outside in the rain!

Lucille and Louise didn't have to help even though they was old enough to pitch in. They was older than us and the most the girls ever did was pick cotton when school was out. They hardly missed ten days of school through the year. They didn't have to work too much. Me and Peter did most of the work and missed most of the school year. That's how we was raised. The man was supposed to do the hard labor and the woman was supposed to take care of the house. Me and Peter was boys but we doing a man's work!

Louise and Lucille head to school in their little dresses and me and Peter would head to the field in our bib overalls. If it be cold out we wear shirts but if not, just the overalls. We eat eggs and bacon almost every morning. Most time we head to the field early. Mama and Minnie Mae bring our food to us after she get the girls out the house. She bring a thermos of hot coffee to daddy. We wasn't allowed to drink coffee. Daddy say, "You can't have no coffee because coffee make you blacker."

I ask daddy, "Why you drinking it?"

He say, "Because I'm grown boy!" That be the end of that. I know not to talk back to daddy.

Mama bring us milk or water and orange juice. That was the orange juice come frozen in a can and is mixed with water to make it. I guess mama mixed a lot of water because it was always pretty weak. But it's what we had and we appreciated it. Whatever you appreciate always tastes good.

We milked our own cows. We get fresh milk and sweet cream butter from those cows. After they is milked, mama shave the top cream off and put it in a jar. Mama have all of us take turns shaking the jar. We line up and pass it back and forth down the line. We shake the jar for about thirty to forty minutes. When a huge chunk of butter formed in the jar, it be time to stop shaking it. Mama take it from the jar and make pats of butter. It was the best sweet cream butter I ever had! It made some of the best cakes I ever had too.

Mama made cakes that people don't even make today; four layers and about eight inches high. Mama made chocolate, coconut, pineapple, German chocolate. Some of the best cakes you ever want to eat! Back then most cakes was made from scratch. Fresh eggs from the hens, milk from the cows, flour from the mill, and most all fresh ingredients. I remember the old rotary egg beater mama used. Wasn't no electric mixers. If there was we didn't have one. No, you had to hold the wooden top with one hand and turn a wooden handle with the other so the steel beaters go around and whip the batter. We had that egg beater for a long time. I wish I still had it.

Grandma taught all her girls how to cook and bake. That's how mama learned. Holiday time there be one table with nothing but all kinds of cakes, sweet potato pies, coconut pies, and sweet potato pudding. Sweet potato pudding is a mix of butter, sugar, cinnamon, nutmeg, with added milk we get fresh from the cow. Not much difference from a pie but it's softer and don't have a crust.

Minnie Mae makes the best sweet potato pudding now. To this day, every time I tell her I'm coming to Baltimore I ask her to make me a sweet potato pudding.

We loved all the Holidays. We knew what mama be cooking; navy beans, collard greens, buttermilk biscuits. Very rare did we have turkey or roast beef. We have barbeque rabbit, barbeque squirrel or chicken. Sometimes daddy roast a coon that he kill while out hunting. That was good eating! Now I can't stomach coon. One day my brother was cooking coon. He had three coons in a big stew pot simmering on the stove. I lifted the lid and all I see was three heads looking up at me. I saw teeth and holes where the eyes was supposed to be. That turned me off to coon. I know people that still go coon hunting. I won't eat it to this day.

We usually have ham on Christmas. Every year around October it be hog killing time. Everyone on the farm get together and slaughter the hogs. Me, Peter, Johnny, Joe, daddy and Mr. Quincy gather by the sty and wait. While the hogs are feeding and not paying attention, daddy and Mr. Quincy cock their rifles and shoot the hogs right between the eyes. After they shoot the hogs, they move them from the sty and cut the throats. Then we load the hogs on the wagon and bring them to the house.

We have a sixty gallon drum, filled half way with water, sitting in a fire pit in the yard. When the water gets real hot and start to boil, we take the hog and pull him up and down in the boiling water about four or five times. Then we turn it over and do the other side about four or five times. We pull the hog out the water and scrape the hair off with our bare hands. Sometimes we use a wood chip. It be a little cold that time a year so you have to pull it off fast or the hair get hard. We hang the hogs from their hind legs on an outdoor rafter. It was hard work but we had to do it.

Daddy and Mr. Quincy gut the hogs. They separate the hearts and chitterlings. Mama, Miss Victoria and the girls clean the chitterlings. Chitterlings are the intestines of the pig. They pull the intestines over a stick and pull it inside out to empty it of all the insides. Then they dump the intestines in a big tub of water with a lot of salt. They let them soak overnight. Next day the women pull the intestines through their hands until the rest of the crap come out. The intestines be soaked one more time. This intestine skin be used to make link sausage or chitterlings.

Back then our hogs was fed our leftover food scraps. Mama kept a slop bucket next to the sink and all the scraps from meals would go in that. That's what we feed the hogs. Farm animals was a lot healthier back then. They wasn't mistreated or kept caged up tight together either. They was in a pen but with room to roam.

After all the insides is taken out the men cut the hog up in sections. They separate the ham from the shoulder, the ribs, loin, and other parts: pig feet, pig knuckles, pig ears. We ate it all. The fat is cut off to make crackling and lard. The lard come from the fat of the pigs. We cut the fat off the pig and throw it to the side. After all the fat off, we cook it in the wash pot. The fat rise to the top and we strain it and dip the crackling out of the grease. We take the grease and pour it into a big round five gallon pail. The grease turns hard and a very light tan. We put all the left over fat, which we called crackling' into another pail. It was called crackling because it was in little chunky pieces. We call it cracklin with no "g" but if you not from the south you can call it crackling.

To make cracklin bread you mix a handful of cracklin with corn meal, egg and a little water. Stir it around 'til its mixed real good. Take a big serving spoon and pour it into a hot frying pan with a little bacon drippings or lard. We had a big black cast iron skillet. Mama brown the mix on both sides. It was good eating. Mama bring cracklin bread and coffee to daddy and us sometimes when we working in the fields. Sometimes she bring us shortening bread. Shortening bread is made the same way as crackling bread but with buttermilk and flour. Mama's food always made the hard work out in the fields a little easier.

Daddy used to make ash cake. Ash cake was like shortening bread but instead of cooking it in the skillet it was cooked in the fireplace. Daddy push back the hot wood ashes until he got to the brick floor of the fireplace. He put the flour bread on the brick and cover it with the wood ashes. He let that cook about thirty minutes. Then he take it out and brush off all the ashes. The house be smelling like fresh bread all day long.

Sometimes daddy boil whole collard green leaves for about five minutes. When he take them out the pot we let the water drip off of them. We sprinkle a little salt on them, hold the whole leaf over our mouths and gobble them down. We used to take cabbage and cut the big leaves off to get it down to the head. We split it four ways, sprinkle a little salt on it and eat the wedge raw. I remember those days and I smile. Days like that made not going to school worth it.

All of those vegetables we grew ourselves; carrots, collards, cabbage, sweet potatoes, white potatoes, turnips, kale, mustard greens, butter beans, snap peas. We grew just about everything. All us had to work in the garden. If we didn't grow it, we wasn't gonna eat. Mama used to can and jar a lot of things. She send her sisters and mama home with a few jars when they visit but most of it was for us.

Lucille was the sister in the kitchen most learning how to cook. Louise never was a cook. Lucille was always the cook. If we was in the field working mama send Lucille to the house to start lunch or dinner. Mama stay in the field with us to make sure everybody work. You know what they say, "When the cat's away the mice will play!" And that's what we do when mama and daddy not out there with us. We was young. As hard as life was, me and Peter still tried to have fun.

Daddy didn't work in the field like we did during cotton picking season. He could shake some peanuts but he wasn't a cotton picker. He said he was too tall. You have to bend down to pick cotton. Everyone else picked the cotton. My fingers would be sore to the touch and blood raw on the tips. Mama put salve and Band-Aids on my fingers for at least the first two weeks. They be pretty raw but I couldn't let the blood or the pain stop me from doing what needed to be done. We had to work so I had to get used to it. I didn't have a choice. Six years old and I didn't have a say. I was a child and children obeyed their parents. If they tell me jump, I jump. If they tell me to pick cotton, then that's what I have to do.

On the rainy days that I went to school, me and Peter leave out with Lucille and Louise. Mama tell us, "Y'all better mind your sisters—you hear me?"

"Yes mama, we hear you." Me and Peter say.

We walk about half a mile from the house to get to the main road. You couldn't see the house from the road. A hill of trees and thick brush hid the house. That's where we stand and wait for the bus. It was a regular yellow school bus like they have today. In Norfolk we walked to school.

Enfield Elementary High School went from the first grade to the twelfth grade. We lived in Enfield for about three years. I only went to school about six months out of those three years. I stayed in the same grade all three years. I get my report card and see, Fail, Fail, Fail. I was a child. I still couldn't read. I didn't know what the word mean but I know I wasn't gonna go to the next grade.

When me and Peter did go to school, the first thing Louise and Lucille did after school is make sure everyone was together. They come get me and Peter from our class and we go to the bus stop. We always be in front of them where they could see us. They be the last to get off so as to make sure nobody got left on the bus. They were responsible for us. That's how it was in big families back then. The older ones was responsible for the younger ones. If anything happened when you was in charge, you have to answer to it. They wasn't letting nothing happen to us. They was good big sisters. They only had to watch us a few times anyway because most sunny days, we was working on Mr. Fleetwood's farm.

Mr. Fleetwood's farm was the first farm I lived on. I was about six years old when I first learned how to plow a mule. First I have to go to the stable and tack the mule. The mule would hold his head down so I could put the bridle on. That's how small I was— the mule had to lower his head for me to reach. After that I hook the mule to the plow. I remember daddy taking me and setting me up at the plow. I steer the mule while he was behind me holding the plow straight so it wouldn't turn over the whole crop. If I don't hold the handle straight it would tear up the crops. I learned quick to hold the reign so the mule stay straight! After I did it for so long the mule knew how to go straight on his own. Sometimes the mule pass gas or do number two. It smelled horrible! They don't stop for a bathroom break. They do it as you going down the row. If you step in it, oh well. It was hard work for a six year old boy. I should have been in school but instead I had to break the land.

The first crop I ever plowed was peanuts. The land had to be tilled first before planting could be done. We had two mules pulling a double plow. After the land was turned over there was a lot of lumps. We run a disc harrow over the land to break up the lumps and smooth out the land. All this work makes the mules thirsty so we give them water in the morning before we bring them to the field. At noon we unhitch the mules, take them home, feed them and give him more water.

That's when we take a break to drink and eat too. We have water and a bowl of beans. Black-eyed peas, navy, butter beans— beans, beans, beans. Navy beans was my favorite. Mama cook them in a big pot with ham hocks. We had a big kettle that mama made three pounds of beans in. She soak the beans overnight. In the early morning she rinse and cook them over a low heat. When I come home to the smell of beans cooking in ham hocks, my mouth start to water! Not only do we smell the beans in the house, but we smell them before we even get to the house! We could tell what kind of bean mama was cooking from the way the air smell. We be fifty yards away and tell if black-eyed peas or butter beans was boiling in the kettle. The black eyed peas had more of a deep, earthy smell and the butter beans had more of a sweet smell. Mama always seasoned the beans with pork so that smelled the same no matter what she was cooking. The smell fill up the outside air like she cooking over an open fire in the yard.

The pork was always smoked using the same kind of wood. Daddy used red oak. We used to have a smokehouse with a heater in it. That's where daddy smoked parts of the hog. Daddy hang the meat in the rafters of the smoke house. He feed the red oak into a black cast iron stove. Daddy come back and forth to make sure enough wood stay in the stove. The smokehouse had to stay a certain heat for the meat to cure and to get the smoke flavor. He feel the meat to see when it's ready. It usually take a few days to cure it. Once it's cured, you can keep it for awhile.

We always had biscuits with our beans. Mama serve the beans with a big pan of sweet buttermilk country biscuits. Fresh milk from the cow made everything smell and taste better. It was cleaner, sweeter. It's hard to describe. But if you had a mama or grandma that made sweet cream buttermilk biscuits then you know what I mean! Ain't nothing like it!

Mama had a long flour pan she baked the biscuits on. She always had dough left over so she take the extra dough, press it into a long roll, push it up the sides of the pan and bake it. We call them Long Head John Pierce. We give them that name because there was a man that lived next to my grandma and the biscuit looked like his long head. His name was John Pierce. We always wanted those biscuits too. As mama had more children, she had to add another Long Head John Pierce biscuit to the amount she made because we all wanted one. I don't know what was special about them. They looked like long hot dog rolls but we thought they was the best thing going. When we go to grandma's house and she making biscuits, we yell out, "Grandma, make us a Long Head John Pierce biscuit!" At first she didn't know what we was talking about. After awhile she knew we was talking about her neighbor. She tell us, "You children better not say that when he be around."

Mr. Pierce was a nice man. He used to stay around the house so much we used to call him Grandma's boyfriend. Whenever grandma cook she tell us, "Go get Mr. Pierce for supper." I never knew if there was something between them. I guess it never really mattered. Grown folks business was grown folks business. We was taught to stay out of it.

After lunch was finished, daddy, Peter, me and the mules head back to the fields. We hitch the mules up to the disc harrow. The disc is two large pieces of steel with about thirty blades. The blades turned on top of each other. One disk pushes the dirt one way and the other one pushes it back the other way. That's how the dirt get broken up nice and smooth. Then we had what is called a drag harrow; it was like a big rake. That would smooth out what the disc harrow couldn't smooth out. The land had to be level and smooth before we could plant anything. This we had to do every season, every year while we was working on the farms.

After we left Norfolk there was no more going to the store to buy a lot of food. If we didn't grow it, raise it, hunt it or cook it ourselves, we didn't eat it. We go to the mill and mama buy baby chicks. We take a wagon load of corn in to trade for chicks. The man was getting over on us more than we were getting over on him with the chickens. If we bought one hundred fifty chicks, we end up with about one hundred. The chicks huddle together at night under the heat lamp to keep warm. In the morning some be dead from suffocation.

We had Bantams, Dominique, Rhode Island Red. Bantam chickens were very small and white. Those was the ones that died most. The Dominique was black and white mixed. A Rhode Island Red was dark red, almost burgundy. They were both bigger but still smaller than what you buy in the store today. I couldn't tell you what the difference was between the three kinds. Once they was cooked and put on the table, they all tasted the same—good!

If grandma wanted a chicken to cook and we were going to her house me and Peter have to kill the chicken. We go into the yard with an ear of corn. We shuck the corn and all the chickens come pecking. There be a hundred chickens out in the yard pecking away. That was what you call free-range. They was free roaming chickens. You gonna pay a lot for free roaming chickens nowadays.

Mama tell us which one she want. We grab it by the head and swing it around and around and pop it till the head snap. The head be in our hand and the body be hanging there limp. Sometimes we put them on the chopping block. I hold the wings and legs. Peter hold the head. We stretch it out long. Peter take the axe and chop the head off at the neck. I sling it to the side and it flop around until it stop. That be where the old saying come from…"quit walking around like a chicken with your head cut off." Sometime I don't sling it quick enough and I get blood all over me!

Mama have a kettle of hot water boiling on the stove. She pour the hot water over the dead chicken, lay it on the chopping board and pull off all the feathers. Then she gut it and cut it into pieces. First she cut off the two wings. Next she cut the short thigh and leg. Then she split the breast by cutting it in half down the middle of the breastbone. She break the back off and pull the neck right out. She cooked every part; the liver, gizzard and neck. If the whole family is gonna eat, we have to kill at least three chickens.

Chickens was much smaller back then. An adult hen was two to three pounds. A rooster was about four pounds after you dressed it real good. Back then it took months for a chick to become fully grown. Today you can buy a five pound chicken that grows in weeks. They shoot them up with something of everything. Mama made sure we didn't kill the chickens while they was babies. Every time I think about all the chicken necks I snapped my mouth swells up and I feel sick inside. I can't eat a fresh chicken no more. I killed a lot of chickens as a little boy.

Our house always had air blowing through it. Half our windows was broken. We have to stick rags in the windows to keep cold air from coming in during the winter. The floor boards had cracks so deep that if the wind blew real hard you could actually see the rug lift off the floor. The rug was a sheet of linoleum. We have to lay bricks on the ends of the rug or else it would roll back up on us. Once it was out of place, you could see everything that goes on under the house. We had a hen house but sometimes the hens make way under our house to nest for the night. We could see the chickens under the house from the floor cracks in mama's room and the living room.

We could tell when the chicks was about to lay eggs because they be sitting on the nest. "The hen sitting on the nest!"

Mama say, "Well leave her alone, she hatching."

We go to the nest the next day and see two, three eggs. Two days later, there might be a dozen eggs. Some eggs be brown, some white. When mama make cakes she tell us, "Go get me some brown eggs." Mama said the brown eggs make the best cakes.

Me and Peter liked the animals. We couldn't play with the chickens so we started raising rabbits. Some days we be working in the cotton field and if a rabbit hop past us we chase it down until we catch it.

There are two types of bunnies. The one with the white tail you can't catch. They're too fast. But the brown ones we can catch. We mess with them until they sit on our lap. We let them run around in the yard until they run free.

Sometimes Minnie Mae run around in the yard too. When we moved to Enfield daddy reminded us, "Whatever Minnie Mae has to do, you do it for her." If the cotton is real thick we have to pull up the weeds that grow along side; that is what we call chopping. If she was behind us chopping we have to chop hers and keep up with our own row. Minnie had to go out there sometimes but we had to do her work. We didn't complain. It was our punishment for hurting her. I am reminded of it every time I see her three finger hand.

Daddy was strict. He made sure we didn't repeat the same mistake twice. He punished us by whooping us or giving us extra work to do. I don't know if it ever mattered to daddy that we didn't go to school because he didn't go to school and yet he was making his way through life. Daddy brought us up the way he was brought up. I'm not sure about this because I never known his father. But I think he must have treated us the way his daddy treated him. I don't fault him for nothing. Some of the whoopings I got was because I did something I should not have done. Some was because I was angry and fighting was the only way to let that anger out. Some of them whoopings I don't know why I got them.

Some might read this and think daddy was a bad man but he was just a man doing the best he could. Some might read this book to the end and think that I was a bad man for doing some of the things I did. But I have few regrets. I can't change my past. I can't change who God gave me for a daddy. Don't know that I would if I could. Daddy always made sure we had a roof over our heads and food to eat. I don't ever remember going hungry. I remember getting plenty of whoopings, but we always had a place to lay our heads. And we always had a full belly.

For three long years we worked hard on Mr. Fleetwood's farm. I was nine years old when we planted and harvested our last crop for him with little to show for it. I can't imagine how that was for daddy. To be a grown man working hard and not to see anything for his labor has got to do something to a man. For me, it was three long years with no school. I was leaving Enfield the same way I came to it; not knowing how to read or write. But this I couldn't change. It's just how it was.

I suppose daddy was angry about some things that he couldn't change. Maybe he didn't realize it. I suppose it rubbed off on me because I carried around a lot of anger too. I hate that I never learned how to read or write when I was young. I was angry that I couldn't go to school and learn like most of the other children. I loved school when I went. But when I started to get teased because I stuttered and couldn't keep up with the lessons, I hated to go. I figure I rather be in the fields plowing my mule and chasing bunny rabbits. To this day I think if my daddy never lost his job in

Norfolk, I probably would have had the opportunity to go to school. I probably would have learned how to read and write. No telling what my life would be. I hate that he lost his job.

I hate to admit some things but some things are true long before you realize it. Even in the anger that I felt towards a lot things and a lot of peoples, there was something in me that kept me going. There was something that, even as a child, I knew was gonna be different. I knew a change was gonna come.

CHAPTER THREE
Reap What You Sow

Be not deceived: God is not mocked:
for whatsoever a man soweth, that shall he also reap.
For he that soweth to his flesh of the flesh reap corruption;
but he that soweth to the Spirit shall of the Spirit reap life
everlasting. And let us not be weary in well doing:
for in due season we shall reap, if we faint not.
Galatians 6:7-9

I was nine years old when we moved from Enfield to Seaboard. When we left Enfield we moved from Mr. Fleetwood's farm to George Harris' farm in Northampton County. I wasn't too sad about leaving Enfield. "Maybe I won't have to work as hard" I thought. "Maybe I'll get the chance to go to school more." Whatever the case, we was gonna be closer to grandma and that was a good thing.

We had to walk down the road a little ways to get to grandma's house. We took a shortcut through the woods to get there. We went that way so we don't have to go through the white folks in town. We tried to stay away from most of the white folk back then. They treated us bad. So we cut through the woods and we end up the road away from all the white folk trouble.

There was a stream that ran the woods, slow and crystal clear. It was nice and cold just like we took it out the ice box. We always stopped at the stream to drink the water.

We get to Grandma's house she ask us, "Who that knocking on my door?" She come to the door with a big smile.

"We come to chop your wood Grandma."

We always make sure Grandma has plenty wood to last her. We was the oldest of her grandsons that lived nearby. We made sure we took care of her. She took care of us more than I knew at the time. When the wood was chopped we stay outside and play for awhile and then head home before it get dark. When we get home mama ask, "Where you boys been at?"

"We was at grandma's house chopping wood for her." She asked, we answered, nothing more to say. When mama was satisfied with an answer, she didn't keep on. We get something to eat and wash up for bed.

We wake up in the morning when the birds start chirping, the cocks crow and the cows moo. They usually wake us up at day break. That was our alarm clock on the farm. Mama don't have to tell us when to get up. By now we get up in the morning and we know exactly what we have to do. We start off right where we left off the night before. We do the same back aching work every day until that job is finished. We had to break the land, disc the land, and harrow the land. It was like in Enfield just on a different farm. We plant the same crops as on Mr. Fleetwood's farm; cotton, soybeans, peanuts, wheat, barley, tobacco, corn. Working on George Harris' farm was no different. Only thing different was we had more land to tend.

On George Harris' farm, we grew a lot of peanuts. Peanuts be harvested in the fall like a lot of the other crops. January, February, March we be getting the peanut poles out the field and stack them up beside the barn and get them ready for the next year. The cotton stalks we have to cut them up so that when it's time to break the land all we have to do is run the stalk cutter over them.

Time go by fast on the farm. Seasons come and go. If I went to school three or four days during the winter I was lucky. But what could I learn in only a few days out of the months? Once I got to Seaboard, I knew I wasn't going to school no more. I went for only a few months during the whole three years we lived in Enfield. Only way I wouldn't have to do the same thing living here was if Daddy got a job at the cotton mill. Five and then six kids, you got to be doing something to take care of them. Back then a lot of the families with more than five or six kids were sharecroppers. My family was no exception. Not all the children worked on the farms like me and Peter, but some of them did.

By now I had missed so much school that it started to be a joke with the other kids. I still stuttered. I missed so many lessons I couldn't even keep up with what Minnie Mae tried to teach me. The children teased me when I did go to class. I preferred to work in the fields over being teased in school and getting into fights all the time. At least I know what I be doing in the fields. That was my school. I learned about life in the fields. Those lessons I took with me through life.

When the spring weather heat up the ground it be time for us to get busy again. The peanut vines be baled and we feed them to the cows and mules. The animals step on the vines and manure and it build up into a thick pile of mess that we use as fertilizer. When it build up so much we go in and shovel it into wheelbarrows and load it onto the sleigh. Then we roll that out and throw the manure in the spreader and put it across the field. We always spread other fertilizer too. It come in big burlap bags with the numbers 10-10-10 wrote across it. I know if I saw those numbers it was fertilizer and we mix it into the dirt before we plant. Then there was the big bag of soda. The word S-O-D-A be written on it. I didn't know what it mean but I know when I saw those letters in that order, it meant I was supposed to spread it on the land too. This had to happen every spring before we start planting.

When planting season start, we work harder than any little child need to work. It was hard work for a man let alone a nine year old boy. But this was my life and I had to do what I had to do. I was never given a choice. I wasn't given a choice to not go to school and I wasn't given a choice to work in the fields. God bless the child who don't have no choice.

We start with picking and baling cotton. We take it to the gin after all the work done. That's when me and Peter get candy from the store. We go to Seaboard Drugstore and buy these long hot candy sticks. They cost a penny apiece. We get a nickel's worth. We buy what we want and we get on out of there! Being colored and going in to town was not easy! We suck on them in the fields when we go picking cotton. We couldn't stop work just because we hungry so while we picking we pop candy in our mouth to kill the hunger spell. We make sure when we left the store on a Saturday we have those hot candy sticks, sugar babies, sugar daddies, and squirrel nuts.

When we take the cotton to the gin, they don't give us money. No, they just give us a receipt. We take the receipt to daddy and he give it to Mr. Harris. We never know how much a bale of cotton bring, all you know was how many bags or bales you carried there. We never know how much Mr. Harris got for all our hard work. The only way we know how much a bale of cotton was if we overheard someone talking about how much it cost. We never got our rightful share. But anytime we shook peanuts and harvested them for Mr. Harris, we go back and pick up the rest of the peanuts from the vine and keep them.

The peanut picker be in the field and we feed the vines into the picker. The vines go one way and the peanuts come out through the hopper into a big metal tub. When the tub fills, we pour them into the burlap peanut sack. Once the bag is full we shape it up and take a long needle and thread, pull the needle through the top of the bag back and forth and back and forth until it's closed up. It won't be coming loose after that. Then when we finish picking peanuts we move the picker to another spot. In the area under the hopper there be a lot of peanuts. At the end of the day the trucks come and we load all the bags on the truck and they take the peanuts to the market. Later we take all the peanuts that fall out of the hopper and fill a bag. Then we hide the bag under the vines. When night comes, we run back to the fields and pull the peanut bag from under the vines and bring it to the house. Mama boil or roast some and daddy take the rest to the market and sell them. We go back into the field and scratch the vines for the rest of the peanuts.

If Mr. Harris saw us picking up peanuts it was okay for us to sell them. But if he didn't see us and we went to sell them then there might be trouble because he say we stole them. I tell you, if you live on the farm you learn how to survive. Thirty acres of peanuts yield about five to six hundred bags. That's how we measured whether we had a good crop. If it was as many bags as the previous year, we had a good crop. If it was less, it was a bad year. It all depends on how much rain fell. Peanuts need rain. If there is a dry spell, they won't grow as well. So we know if we had a good harvest or not. But we never got any money for it.

We scrap the corn the same way. After the corn be harvested we go through the field to get the extra corn that we leave out there. Daddy split what we leave out there into bags. We take that to the mill and sell it. We hope that we getting the same price that Mr. Harris got for the same corn but we never knew. We couldn't question it either. If we question it, they know we probably stole it. Then we do the same thing with the scrap cotton. Sometimes we have over a thousand pounds of scrap cotton. Daddy had to be careful about how he take it to the mill or else it raise suspicion. It was hard and it wasn't fair. But it was payback for the money we didn't get at the end of the year when our debt got settled. Even as a child I know it wasn't fair. And even though it made me who I am, I don't wish that hard or unfair a life on nobody.

We grow soybeans for Mr. Harris, but that was a crop we couldn't salvage for ourselves. Sugar cane we kept. That was some hard work. We go to the field and sickle it, put it on the sleigh and bring it to the barn. Then we hook the mule to the grinder and he pulls it in a circle. As it come around we put the sugar cane through the press. The stem go out one end and the juice run back into a tub. When the tub get full, we pour it into a big old cast iron wash pot and cook it. There be a sweet, sugary smell in the air. Imagine the smell of cotton candy at the carnival. That's how the hot cane juice smells—sugary sweet!

Later in life I had my father's great grandmother's cast iron wash pot. It was huge. It was passed down four generations. I was the fifth generation to hold that pot. I had it until New Jersey in the late seventies. Whenever I used it and finished with it I would take it and flip it over next to the garage. That's when it was stolen. I was walking in the back yard one day and realized, "my pot is gone!"

There was a six inch crack at the top of the pot. Whenever I cooked in it I wouldn't fill it past that point. I can remember cooking in that pot. Mama also washed clothes *and* cooked in that pot. She fill the pot with boiling water and put in a little oxen soap. Then the clothes would go in. She used a big paddle to stir the clothes around until they were clean.

Just like grandma's fish fries, daddy threw parties and he fry chicken and fish in those same pots. He invite peoples from all over the county. Two pots we use to fry chicken and fish. Mama used one pot for the fish and one pot for the chicken. One of those pots had just cleaned our clothes earlier in the day.

I remember the first washing machine mama ever got. It was like a tub on four legs that she kept on the porch. She was in heaven because she didn't have to use that cracked wash pot anymore. I said if I ever saw that cracked pot I know it mine but I never did see it again. It was a long time before I could tell daddy it was missing. One day we got to talking and I slipped it in. "Daddy, you know somebody stole Big Momma's pot?"

"Did I hear you say somebody stole momma's pot?"

"Yes sir, I did." Daddy mumbled a little something under his breath but that was the end of it. Nothing else was ever said about that pot, at least not between the two of us.

Big momma was daddy's mother. She wasn't right in the mind but she was a good woman. I don't know why they call her big momma because she was tall and thin. Every other month daddy pick her up from the mental hospital and bring her home to visit. Sometime he pick her up so she can help us harvest the crops and help us around the farm. She loved to feed the pigs and milk the cows. Some time she come to help mama have her babies. She was like a midwife. I loved having Big Momma around.

She was always so happy to see us. She had a lot of strange ways but that's what made her special. You know years ago when someone wasn't right in the mind the good folk used to say "they special". Big Momma really was special.

There was absolutely no running through the house! She was very clean and expect the house to stay clean. We know to fall into place when Big Momma come around. In other words, straighten up and fly right because Big Momma don't take no mess! We knew she loved us even when it didn't seem like it. Whenever she was confused or upset about something she go to sweep the yard. Yes, she actually have a real broom and sweep the yard! We had a lot of fun with her. Sometimes she give us candy and cookies. When she was in a playful mood she say, "Who is your pappy, your hair is so nappy, but great god you is one ugly child!" She didn't mean nothing by that. Besides, our pappy was her son! We always laughed. But we always cry when she leave.

Yes, I remember all that stuff. I remember all the peoples who was there in my life with a laugh or a hug, a firm hand, a switch or a thick leather belt.

Yes, Big Momma's old wash pot cooked a lot of love and cleaned a lot of life. Mama had a skillet and pot that she cooked smaller meals in. With a family of eight I don't know if any of our meals was small! I loved when mama made chicken pot pie. She use the back and the wing for the pot pie. The backs and wings were poor folk pieces back then. Now a wing cost more than a breast! Mama make a ball out of flour and water and roll it around until it get real thick. She sprinkle black pepper and salt and roll out more until it get real thin. Then she take the knife, cut it into strips, and lay it onto the whole pieces of the chicken. She let it simmer down and then come back and put another layer of dough and let it cool down and thicken up. Some people call it chicken and dumplings but we called it chicken pot pie because she rolled the dough out. The skin on the chicken turns the dough and liquid into thick, yellow-like stew. That's what made it so good.

Salt and pepper was used for everything. Food was fresher because we raised our own. That's why it tasted better. Chicken stew, or what we called chicken Brunswick, was chicken, peas, butterbeans, corn, carrots, and white potatoes cut into little small pieces. Add everything but the potatoes and let them simmer down for about an hour and a half. Then about ten minutes before it's done, dump your potatoes in there and stir it up. Mama served that with hot biscuits or fried cornmeal.

Mama served us on tin plates. She had dinner plates but only used those for company. We ate off the tin plates because if we dropped them on the floor they wouldn't break. The food was so good I'd lick my plate and put the empty tin on top of my head. Why I did that I don't know. I was a child. But I will always remember mama's cooking. I ate until we didn't have no more. Daddy say, "Woman, this damn boy done ate so much his stomach is under the table!"

At nine I could tell you anything about the food I ate, the vegetables we grew, the animals we raised but I still couldn't read or write. I don't know that I ever paid much attention to others being able to read. Then one day my cousin Junior was visiting and I realized he was reading a book. I heard him say words out loud as he followed along on the pages. I know he was reading because I heard him talking out loud as he looked at different books and things. I'd see and hear others reading from books. It was a sinking feeling—knowing I was not doing something the other children who went to school was doing.

The few times that I did go to school, little girls would pass notes to me. I take the note and stick it in my shirt pocket. Later I go to my cousin and ask him to read it to me. Sometimes they say sweet things. Sometimes they say mean things. I always have my cousin or sister write something back.

I look at those little notes or a book and not even know those letters was letters never mind words. I didn't learn my ABCs until I was around twelve. My sister helped me learn my letters. I only learned how to say them. I still didn't recognize an A as an A or B as a B. I never saw those letters on my report card. I know D and F wasn't good. I didn't know that if you put letters together it make a word. Singing the alphabet song was the best I could do.

At ten years old, I still couldn't read any of the books I was given in the first grade. If I was reading in school the kids tell me the wrong words to say then they make fun of me. I repeat what they tell me. The teacher ask me, "Does that look like the word I asked you to read?" If I said the wrong word, the teacher reach over two desks and hit me with a long switch. They kept those long switches in the corner of the room. By the time we got outside I'd be so mad I start a fight with the boy that gave me the wrong word to say. I couldn't go home and tell on the teacher that took a switch to me. If I said "Mama, the teacher whooped me today" I'd get another whooping for saying so.

"Well what the teacher give you a whooping for?" Mama ask.

"I got whooped for saying the wrong word and for fighting."

"Well I got nothing to do with that." Mama say.

Then I'd get expelled. It didn't matter much because I wouldn't be in school no way. I didn't always get in trouble. I stopped saying words that the other kids tell me. Then I got smart. I decided to tell the truth. When the teacher ask me, "Aron, did you study your lessons last night?"

"No ma'am." I say.

"Why didn't you study Aron?"

"Well ma'am, I had to get wood in for the night after school" I would explain. "Then I had to tend to the mules. Then I had to work in the fields 'til nightfall." It was hard to tell the truth but it was even harder to go back to school the next day knowing I didn't fit in. I knew I didn't know the lessons. I knew I'd be teased. I'd probably get in a fight. I'd probably get in trouble again. The teacher used to tell me, "I got mine. Now you got to get yours. I'm here to teach you if you want yours."

She was right. I had to get mine—but how? They never had the time to spend with me alone because the class had over forty students. The classroom had a good eight to ten rows of six desks each. It was overcrowded. There was no air conditioning. The teachers didn't always act kind to me. I suppose now I understand. The white school had air conditioning. They had new books and their furnace worked in the winter. We had the kind of furnace that the janitor had to come to early morning and dump coals in it.

That's how we got our heat. Sometimes it worked, sometime it didn't.

Me and Peter used to love the time of year when school was about to close for the summer. They used to have May Day at the end of the year. Every class had to do something for May Day. The girls would plait the pole with different colors of tissue paper streamers. Every class put on different acts. I never had the chance to participate in anything like that but I loved watching the boys play baseball and tag. Report card time would come around I'd only have Ds and Fs. My sister would bring mine home because I'd be in the field. I come home at the end of the day and mama or one of my sisters say, "You know you have to repeat the same grade?" After awhile I figured, why bother? I knew what I had to do in the fields and I wasn't graded on it.

Life wasn't always unfair—just sometimes. I remember daddy wanted a car about a year in working for George Harris. He be on the lot looking and looking. He had his eye on one in particular so he talks to the man and told him, "I want that car." They shake hands and it was a deal. Daddy got a 1953 green four door Packard. He was proud of that car! The car dealer calls George Harris.

"I got one of your hands down here wanting to buy a car."

George Harris verify that daddy worked on his farm. Mr. Harris paid for the car. Daddy have to work for nothing the whole year or more until the car was paid for. No matter how long it take, you gonna pay for that car out of your share. Trouble was daddy's share was never what it supposed to be.

By the time the crops was harvested on one hundred fifty acres we knew that should be a lot of money. If a bale of cotton weigh five hundred pounds that mean you stuffed more than twice that to end up with that much. If one bale brought two hundred or two hundred and fifty dollars and you pick fifty or sixty bales, you know that was a lot of money. And that was just for one crop! The money suppose to be split between daddy and Mr. Harris. But out

51

of our half daddy have to pay for the seed, the other workers and every other expense or debt, including the car. At the end of the year Mr. Harris settle daddy's debt and daddy might get five hundred dollars if he lucky. Most times he wouldn't get that.

When my cousins come down from Norfolk to visit I see how they is living. Some that leave and come back years later come back driving fancy cars. They go to Norfolk for jobs and come home with money in their pockets. They come back wearing nice clothes. Daddy wear bib overalls or khakis. He had one pair of shoes for Saturday or Sunday.

But we got ours. Like I said, you learn how to survive. George Harris tell Daddy and my older cousin Woodrow to take the cattle from one pasture to the next. Once they drive the cattle through the pasture, when the last one come through they hit him on the head and kill it.

Daddy tell Mr. Harris, "Well we lost one of them. He just fell dead." Mr. Harris had so many cattle he didn't know or care. We take the bull, hang him up and skin him. Then we split it with the other families on the farm. We didn't eat much beef but when we did we enjoyed it even more!

There was four other families on Mr. Harris' farm. Mr. Ernest lived behind us on the back end of the farm. Mr. Ernest had four kids. His boys went to school. Mr. Ernest's wife had an artificial leg.

Millard Ballmer was our cousin. His wife's name was Honey. They had three boys; Pear, L.C., Millard Jr. They also went to school. L.C. stuttered just like I did. Millard Sr. and Honey didn't get along well. They was always fighting. When she finally had enough of him, she left him and carried all the children away to New York but left junior there. He looked too much like his daddy they say.

Woodrow was Aunt Bea's son. We call him Doc. He was the youngest one with a family on the farm. He was about nineteen with a wife and child. He lived in one of the houses off the main road leading up to our house. Doc was a short dark skinned man with cowlicks in his head. He used to let me hang around him until one day I told his wife that I saw him kissing one of the Powell girls. Then Doc told me, "I won't never take you no place else!" To this day he reminds me of that.

Aunt Bea and Uncle Will lived across the street from us on the Little's farm. Uncle Will and Aunt Bea had four children; Margie Lee and Tittle lived in Norfolk. Ora Mae and Woodrow lived there for awhile too but moved back to Seaboard.

They got paid by the day when they worked. They were tenant farmers. Some people called sharecropping half-sharing. The difference between a tenant farmer and a sharecropper is how you get paid. Tenant farmers got paid by the week. Sharecroppers get paid once a year. The crop supposed to be ours as well as the landowners'. Our pay is supposed to be based on whatever crop is brought in and how much we get for it. When it's time to settle up, all the material, seed, and everything supposed to be split. But most would come out of our share. Nothing would come out the land owners share. So we end up paying for everything and getting very little after it all counted.

When Aunt Bea and Uncle Will finished picking cotton and peanuts on Mr. Little's farm, they come and work for daddy. Daddy paid them when he could. The good thing was daddy didn't have to go and get them. They were on the main road and we could see their house from where we lived. They could walk to the cotton patch or peanut field. Whatever cotton you pick, that's what you get paid for. If they picked a hundred pounds they would get two dollars and fifty cent for the hundred. If the cotton is not as plentiful you might get three dollars per hundred.

One day Uncle Will was working in the field stacking hay. He slipped and fell and got hurt very bad. There was no phone to call an ambulance. Someone picked him up and took him to a hospital in Roanoke Rapids. The doctor came out and told Aunt Bea that Uncle Will was paralyzed. Aunt Bea was heart-broken.

Her granddaughters Barbara Jean and Martha Lee were with her. When they came home I asked Aunt Bea if I could stay with her to help her. She said I have to ask mama. Mama say yes.

It was hard for Aunt Bea to do everything for Uncle Will. He couldn't do anything for himself. Aunt Bea had to feed him, clean and wash him, turn him over and do all his work. I started doing all his work. We had wood stoves so I cut wood and bring it in the house at night. I used to help give him a bath too. I did as much as I could to help her out. I loved all my aunts but Aunt Bea was my favorite. I used to go to Norfolk three or four times a year when she was living. Aunt Bea passed away in 2009 at the age of 101. We buried her in Norfolk. They didn't bring her back home to Seaboard.

Mr. Archie Powell was the fourth family on the farm. He lived in front of us. He had three boys and four pretty girls. I called myself liking Eula. Peter say he was going with Erma. Doc got caught kissing Erma. Well he didn't get caught, I told on him. I was ten. I didn't know no better. Erma was just a teenager. She was big for her age. She didn't like young boys. None of the girls did. They always liked older guys. Even after I told on Doc they still messed around.

Daddy had to be at the tobacco barn all night. It was time to cure the tobacco and the fire had to be stoked so it stay at a certain temperature for the tobacco to dry. Doc used to hang out with daddy at the barn. Erma used to sneak up to the barn where Doc was and they make out on the side of the barn. I never followed them but you knew. Those girls didn't keep nothing to themselves. They thought it was something to talk about. Mr. Powell couldn't do nothing with them girls. They was fast! That's what we call girls that kissed and made out with older boys—fast! They did and said what they wanted to do and say. Mr. and Mrs. Powell drank a lot. That might have had something to do with it, I don't know. Sometimes we think all our troubles gonna be swallowed down with a bottle of liquor. That ain't how it works. You only be drunk with the same troubles. Some peoples go to their graves trying to drown out what's troubling them.

We were the fifth family on the farm. We say farm but it was really a plantation. We lived in a little shotgun house made of grey, weathered clapboard and a rotted out low country front porch. Once the steps rotted away we put concrete blocks there to get up on the porch so we could get in the house. I loved our raggedy tin roof house. When it rained at night and the drops hit that tin roof, boy that was some good sleep. If it rained while we wasn't home, we pray the pot be in place to catch the water from the hole in the roof. It always leaked.

Me, Peter, Big Will, and Red all shared a bed. Big Will was born in Norfolk shortly before we left. Red was born in Seaboard not too long after we moved here. They was the baby boys and didn't have to work in the fields like me and Peter. The four of us shared the bed—two at the top, two at the bottom. If someone wet the bed we all blame it on each other. We play in the bed tickling each other's feet and horse around. Mama and daddy yell to us, "What's going on in that room? Don't make me come in there!"

Grandma, Aunt Alpha and Aunt Eddy used to make quilts for us. Those quilts were so warm! They stuff them with chicken feathers and scrap material. Once and awhile they forget a needle in the quilt and we get stuck during the night. I got stuck plenty of time. The house was cold in the winter. Mama and daddy kept the heater in their bedroom. Sometime, when it was too cold, I open the door so the heat could come through and warm our room.

All the bedrooms was on one side of the porch. The kitchen was on the other side. That was the only thing over there, a big kitchen. We ate on a picnic table. Most everybody we know on the farms had one like that.

All the girls shared a room. When Marianne was born she stay with mama until she got big enough to sleep with the other girls.

During this time Elvis Pressley was a big deal. Daddy said if we work hard that year he get us a TV. So we did and daddy bought one of those big mahogany consoles with the stereo and radio attached to it. We got three channels and played 45s on the record player. Elvis Pressley had sneakers and material with his name on it that they sold at Field's Department Store in Roanoke Rapids. His face was all over the material. The twins worried mama to death about getting this material and those damn white sneakers with his picture on them.

Mama say, "Okay, you pick cotton after school and I'll buy it." So they picked. The twins had to work during cotton picking season. They missed some days of school too during cotton picking season. Mama bought the sneakers and material and made the skirts. We went to town and all the black girls were wearing these big hoop skirts with Elvis Pressley's white face all over them!

A few weeks later it was news spreading that Elvis Pressley said, "The only thing a nigger can do for me is shine my shoes, wear my sneakers and buy my material." I don't know if this is true or not but most black folk believed it. All the girls took those fancy skirts and sneakers and put them in pile and burned them down to ashes. They stopped liking him after that. Years later when he started having blacks in his band and black background singers, they started liking him again.

The girls seem to always dress nice. Me and Peter wore bib overalls most days. Big Will, Red and the girls all went to school. Me and Peter went to the fields. The school bus picks them up and drops them off in front of Aunt Bea's house. Me and Peter walk to and from the cotton patch.

Hundreds of acres of land all worked by black families for little to no money. Each family tended at least twenty five acres. Not us—we tended one hundred fifty. Even though I was young, I couldn't understand how we could work so many acres and not get any money at the end of the year when we settled with Mr. Harris. It didn't matter much to me then because I was young and had to do whatever daddy say do. And we be out in the fields the following year doing it all over again. Me and Peter still be running around playing and working and not really knowing what was going on. As far as school was concerned, if we went we went, if we didn't go, we didn't miss nothing. By now we was so far behind it didn't make no sense for us to go at all.

Sometime me and Peter go shake peanuts on another farm for fifteen cents a stack. We put up about twenty five or thirty stacks of peanuts. We collect about four dollars and split it. That was a lot of money for us at our age and we be happy.

Peter buy candy or ice cream and Erma come around to get some. But that was the only time she hang around. We called Erma Shirley sometimes. Other times we called her "spot on the left jaw" because she had a big light birthmark on her left jaw. She hated that name. The last time I saw her was about fifteen years ago. She had the nerve to ask me "How's my boyfriend doing?" I said, "Oh he your boyfriend now is he?" We just smile.

Erma had a brother named Thurman but Peter used to call him white eye. The white of his eye was so white we couldn't call him nothing else! Nobody went by their real names no how. Back then, everybody was called something else and every boy had themselves a little girlfriend. Mine was Erma's baby sister Eula.

Eula was a fast girl. She didn't want me because I was too young. Like Erma, if I had ice cream or candy she be hanging around. If we was going to town to the cotton mill, they ask us to bring something back. And of course we did. We was the weekday boyfriends. Soon as the weekend hit, they didn't want to be bothered with us. They went for the older boys. They wanted the boys that were driving cars and could get around. Years later when I come to town in my '58 shiny, two door black Chevy Impala they was all over me.

Like I said, the Powell girls were fast and cussed around their parents like soldiers. Mama tell us, "You all can play together if you want but whatever you done heard you better leave it out there! Don't bring that talk home with you."

Sometimes me and Peter forget that we was home and we cuss. Mama hear us and warn, "What I tell you? You better leave that language where you heard it."

One day I was downtown Seaboard smoking a cigarette that Mr. Buddy's son George Washington gave me. Imagine that, George Washington gave me a cigarette! Daddy and some other man was up the road standing next to his car shooting the breeze. I walked up to daddy to get some money. I forgot I was holding the cigarette in my hand. Daddy asked me, "What's that in your hand boy?" I looked down and said "Oh shit!" He gave Peter fifty cents. I knew what I was getting. I was smoking and I cussed! I knew when we get home that night daddy was gonna whoop me old and new! The only thing that saved me was mama talked to him.

"Now Earl, these boys is growing up. They ain't six years old no more. You know they hanging out with older boys. You got to bend a little bit. It better that you knows what they doing before they sneak and burn the house down."

"Well I'm not buying them no cigarettes!"

"I'm not asking you to buy cigarettes. The boys work hard all day in them fields. They making some of their own money to do with as they please. All I'm asking is you bend a little!" Mama was serious when she talked. She was usually a soft spoken women but when she wanted to get her point made, she didn't back down. Daddy shouted up a storm but he didn't whoop me. Mama saved me again. It seem like the older I got the worse the whoopings got. I remember one night getting whooped so bad the skin on my legs broke. Mama put lard on them so I wouldn't stick to the bed sheets. I don't know what I did to ever deserve a whooping that bad.

We started buying ten cent bags of Duke Tobacco. We rolled our own cigarettes. We did that during the week. Weekend come, if we had a dollar, we buy a twenty cent pack of cigarettes. I smoked Kent and Peter smoked Viceroy. We didn't smoke our rolled Dukes around the girls. That was too country. We only wanted them to see us smoking the cigarettes in the pack. That was more sophisticated. Daddy never liked it. He didn't smoke or drink and he didn't want to see us do it either, whether they was rolled or out the pack!

Uncle Jack was a different story! He smoked like a chimney and drank like a fish. He come to live with us in Seaboard shortly after we moved to George Harris' farm. Something had gone wrong at the cotton gin and Uncle Jack lost his job. I remember him bringing cotton to mama so maybe he got fired for stealing! He ended up working with us on the farm.

Uncle Jack was a tall, thin man with dark skin and a bald crown. He never wore a tie, even when he wore a suit but he always looked real nice when he got dressed. He used to keep watch over us when mama and daddy had somewhere to go. I was always the one to get in trouble whenever mama and daddy was out of the house. Mama used to tell Uncle Jack, "No matter what you do, put your belt on Paul's behind if he acts up!" Uncle Jack was the type person who smiled as he told you not to do something. I would test him. I'd either fight one of my sisters or brothers or do something I wasn't supposed to do. He whooped me about three or four times for acting out. I learned my lesson after that.

Every Wednesday, Uncle Jack go to see his girlfriend. He always ask us to sweep out daddy's car and clean it up. We siphon gas from the tractor so he have enough to get to town. He give us a nickel or dime for cleaning the car. Sometimes he don't give us nothing but he bring cookies or candy home. He pick up Miss Pauline and they go to the drive-in-movies.

Sometimes, Uncle Jack go into town with daddy's car and have too much moonshine. His drink of choice was white lightning. He stay with Miss Pauline until he sober up. He know daddy was crazy about his car and he didn't want to damage it. Uncle Jack didn't have no license to drive so you know he and daddy must have been good with each other. Daddy loved him like a brother. And

Uncle Jack loved daddy. Six in the morning and Uncle Jack be right back on the farm ready to work.

Uncle Jack was spoiled. He was the only boy out of seven girls that grandma had. He always knew what to do to get over. He might be sitting around looking like he lost his best friend in the world. His sisters come up handing him money just to cheer him up. He run out the house and go up the road to get moonshine. He be out drunk and get into a scuffle. Sherriff Dillard Druid take Uncle Jack straight off to jail. That's where he stay until the next day when daddy and grandma come to Jackson to bail him out.

One day Uncle Jack was over grandma's house cooking. He was frying fat back and the grease was just a popping. He told us to stop running through the house—to go outside and play. Louise didn't listen. She ran into the stove and a pan of hot grease spilled all over her face. I was outside playing with the other neighborhood kids when all of a sudden we hear this loud scream come from the house. It was Louise. We didn't know what happened so we stayed outside playing. Uncle Jack ran out the house carrying Louise. Then we know it must be bad. He took her to Dr. Parker's office downtown Seaboard.

Dr. Parker looked just like Santa Claus. He was red faced, had a big, fat stomach and he wobbled when he walked. He actually used to play Santa Claus at the white school. He had his office right beside the drug store. He cleaned up the burn and put Genuine Black and White ointment on it. That's what it's called; Genuine Black and White ointment. That ointment is dark and real thick. It smells like turpentine. You can still buy it today.

When she come back to the house she had a big bandage on her face. Mama and daddy felt bad this happened but they always tell us to listen. If you don't listen, you got to suffer with the consequences.

When it was time to dress the burn again grandma dressed it in the same Genuine Black and White ointment and covered it in gauze. Once the rawness went away and the skin turned white she run a stick of cocoa butter over the skin every day until it healed. You can barely tell that she was burned. If you saw it you might think it was a birthmark or something. To this day, Louise wears a bang over that side of her face to cover the area where she was burned and where part of her hair didn't grow back.

Grandma could do everything. She had a remedy for everything. One time I had ringworm. Grandma take the juice of her snuff and rub it on the spot. The ringworm was gone in a couple days. Another time, I was about to break out with the chicken pox. Grandma bake yellow cornmeal until it turned brown. She put me in the bath and dry me off real good. Then she rub the baked cornmeal all over me 'til my skin turn white and ashy. It took away the itch and the chicken pox.

Mama told me a story once. One time, before I was born and mama pregnant with the twins, the family travelled to see grandma. While they was there, mama went into labor. They rushed her to Roanoke Rapids Hospital to have the babies. They saved Lucille but Louise didn't make it. Daddy put dead Louise in a shoebox and drove back to Grandma's house. Grandma took one look at Louise's stiff body and went to work. She grabbed a silver foot tub and told daddy, "Go fill this up with cold water." Daddy know not to question grandma when she taking care of business. She warmed up the wood stove. She took Louise's lifeless body and dipped her in the cold tub water. Then she wrapped that baby girl in a towel and put her in the stove, took her out, and blew in her mouth. Then she repeated the same thing three more times; cold water, stove, blow in the mouth; cold water, stove, blow in the mouth. I don't know if she was praying or what but after the third time, the baby start moving! Daddy saw this and started to move toward her. Grandma yelled, "I got this Earl!" Daddy say, "If you save her Miss Ora, she your baby." Well she did save the baby and daddy changed his mind. He took the baby, wrapped her up in a blanket and took her back to hospital. The doctors couldn't believe their eyes. And mama nearly fainted with shock! Louise lived!

She is grandma's special grandchild. Mama had another set of twins, Marianne and Martha Anne. Martha Anne died at birth too but grandma couldn't save her. Grandma was something else. She was a miracle worker. But she couldn't save Martha.

It seemed like Grandma worked all the time. I don't know how she did all that she did. Back then, everybody worked hard. It was a hard life for poor black folk in the south. Life stays hard until you is able to do better. I always said I was gonna do better. I didn't know how and I didn't know when but I always said once I got a job and did better, I was gonna have nice clothes and nice cars. I reminded myself of that all the time. When I saw someone dressing the way I thought I want to dress or driving a car I thought I want to drive, something in me said I was gonna have it one day. I couldn't read or write but I knew how to work. I knew that hard work would get me something out of life one day. I didn't think not being able to read or write was gonna stop me. I knew what I wanted and that was it. Nothing else mattered to me back then. As I got older, after a while it didn't matter to me whether I could read, write or go to school. After a while all I wanted to do was dress nice.

Grandma worked in the white school kitchen during the day and in the white homes in the evening. She used to bring home pimento cheese and peanut butter and jelly sandwiches that was left over from lunch. Whatever was left she bring it home. Sometime she have a sack full of sandwiches on her shoulder. After school, almost every day during cotton season time, she walk humped over three, four miles with that big sack slung over her shoulder so everybody in the fields have something to eat. On the weekend we take what she bring home on Friday so we have something to eat on Saturday and Sunday. Grandma really was the backbone of the family. Daddy thought a lot of her. Everybody thought a lot of her.

Saturday was a big night for the family at Grandma's house. She have us go downtown to the fish market to get butterfish and whiting. Fish was fifteen cents a pound back then. We buy about twenty pounds of fish. Everybody chipped in to buy the fish. Grandma fry up a batch of fish and serve it with potato salad, pork and beans and coleslaw that she bring home from the school. I like to think she made those beans special for me. We have a loaf of white bread and we make fish sandwiches using only white bread and fish—no ketchup or hot sauce. One thing is for sure, Grandma always make sure Mr. Long Head John Pierce was there to eat with us.

When I was young, grandma was the only person I knew that always had money. If she was ever broke she never let me know about it. Whenever I ask her for a nickel or dime, she had it to give. I heard someone say, "Grandma hold a dollar until Lincoln holler!" Mama ask her for a couple of dollars on loan and she always have it. Grandma know we had the hardest time out of all her children so she made sure we was taken care of. She really stuck by us. She bought all our Holiday clothes at Fields Department Store or Montgomery Ward. She brought us food while we picked cotton. She bailed Uncle Jack out of jail. She saved Louise. Yes, Grandma meant the world to us.

After she worked in the school kitchen, she cleaned the white folk houses. Sometimes she do that two or three hours each day after school. They pick her up and bring her home. The white folk, even the younger ones say, "Okay Ora, we'll see you tomorrow." We could never call an older person by their first name but them white folk had no problem doing it. But you better believe it don't matter how old grandma was or how young they was, grandma say, "Yes sir and Yes ma'am, Miss this or Mr. that." She didn't call them by their first name.

Grandma was the peace maker. Grandma always knew if something was wrong with one of her children. If there was something going on, she knew about it and she help them fix it. She sit husband and wife both down at the table and she get to the bottom of what's going on. She take that dip of snuff in her lip and she get to talking and spitting and she straighten things out. You hear me, she fix things. Grandma was the type of women that could fix anything.

One Saturday when me, Peter, my cousin Prince and James Wallace went into town we got into a scuffle. These six white boys drove up on us, jumped out of their pickup truck and yelled out, "Niggers, what you doing in my town?"

It was five of them white boys and four of us. We weren't scared. All we know is we had to fight if we want to get home. You know what they say, "When your back is up against the wall, there ain't nothing to do but come out swinging!" Everything happened real fast after that. Peter happened to have a big stick in his hand. I don't know when he got it or how long he had it but he knocked one of the boys out cold! By then we was all in a battle. When they realized they wasn't gonna win they picked up the kid that Peter knocked out, jumped in the truck and drove back to the farm.

We knew the boys. One was the farm owners' son and the other three was his buddies. Before we knew it, everyone knew about the fight. Then Cal Gay come around to talk to Grandma. Grandma explained, "Now Sir, your boys done start the trouble. I suspect you don't want me to whoop them boys for starting trouble do you?"

"Now Ora, we gonna take care of this" Cal Gay say. He took them boys home and took care of it. We saw them downtown the following Saturday and we didn't have no problem with them. I don't know what else Grandma said or done, but we never had no trouble out of those white boys again.

Some Saturdays we go downtown to the movie theater. One day, about six of us went to the movies. The white folks was on the first floor and we was in the balcony. Sometimes some of the black kids buy soda and pour it down on the white folk head. I did my share of wrong but I never did that! My problems come from my temper. I didn't go looking for trouble but trouble seem to find me. I guess pride keep me from never backing down.

This particular Saturday, I fell asleep in the movie. Everybody left and they had no idea that I was still sleeping in that chair. When they got home, mama and grandma asked them, "Where Paul?" Mama say everybody look around at each other like deer in headlights. It wasn't long before Grandma realized that they left me in the movie theater. When daddy come home he carried grandma to the man who operates the movie theater, Mr. Phillip. By now it was about eleven o'clock at night. When grandma went to Mr. Phillip door, he asked, 'Who there?"

"Mr. Phillips, it's me, Ora Jennings!" He knew grandma. Everybody knew grandma and nobody bothered with her or gave her trouble.

"I think you locked one of my boys in the movie house."

Nobody argued with grandma. They just went down to the movies and Mr. Phillip went upstairs and there I was, fast asleep.

"I got him Ora!" Mr. Phillip yelled downstairs to grandma. "Here he is!"

Mr. Phillip woke me up and I'm wondering what should happen that this white man is standing over me. Last I knew I had gone there with a group of black children and here this white man waking me up. Thank God I didn't wake up before they got there. With the lights out the theater was dark as a moonless night. I would have been scared to death!

Grandma could hold her own with any man. For some reason nobody bothered her. If they did I didn't know about it. Everybody respected grandma and she treated everyone with kind regard. Grandma knew most of the landowners and they treated her better than they treat daddy.

It seems to me that all the white men daddy worked for had some peculiar ways. Mr. Cal Gay was one strange man. He was real tall with a big stomach. He always wore khaki pants, khaki shirt, khaki cap. He drove a green Ford pickup. When we moved to Cal Gay's farm, it was around 1955 and I had just turned twelve. Daddy thought it would be better on his farm than on George

Harris' farm. The farm owners tell you anything just to get you to work for them. The cotton grow the same no matter what farm you on. And the picking don't be no easier. Cal Gay's was no different.

Cal Gay sold daddy a John Deere to use on the farm. That was the good part. Peter taught me how to drive the tractor. I thought I graduated school when I learned how to drive that tractor! When I was first learning how to drive the tractor I drove it straight into the side of the house! But that's how I learned to drive a car—by steering that tractor up and down the fields. I could have died and gone on to heaven because we didn't have to pull the mules as much as we did before. We use the mules sometime to plow the garden. They got to rest a little after we got the tractor. They was tired just like us.

Cal Gay wasn't right. He didn't treat daddy good but sometimes he come to the field with a truck full of cold sodas. Me and Peter go off running to get a Pepsi. Working out in the hot sun we was always thirsty. Mama bring us water and juice sometime, but soda was a treat. We didn't know it then but we paid for them sodas. When it comes time to square off and settle debt at the end of the year, you better believe the sodas be added in. Wasn't nothing free! It was a cruel lesson I learned early in life. Somehow daddy never made more than a few hundred dollars for a whole year's work! And he didn't own the tractor at the end of the year. That was it! When daddy found out he didn't own the tractor after three years of working that really broke daddy down. The John Deere went back to Cal Gay, daddy left for Baltimore in his yellow Buick; we packed up and moved to Uncle Beulah's farm.

Uncle Beulah was a strange man too. He didn't do no social with the black folk if the white man was around. He be smoking and carrying on with the white man and act like he don't know us while they around. Soon as they leave, he hang around us like nothing ever happened. Uncle Beulah was mama's brother-in-law. He owned his land.

One day there was a big mess in town. Uncle Beulah had carried his wife Aunt Eddy to Roanoke Rapids to buy her a winter jacket. That same weekend he carried his girlfriend to the same store and bought her the exact same jacket. Just so happen they both come to town with the same jacket on. I thought Aunt Eddy was gonna back down because she always act scared of Uncle Beulah. But that Saturday, Aunt Eddy, Aunt Teen, Aunt Alpha and Aunt Bea was all there and they was about to go after his girlfriend! She made it to her car and took off! When Aunt Eddy got to grandma's house, she took that jacket off, put it in the wood stove and watched it burn! Uncle Beulah saw another side of Aunt Eddy that day. I don't know if he ever stepped out on her again!

My Aunts didn't take no mess! Grandma didn't raise her girls to take nothing sitting down. When they was backed up against the wall, they fight like the devil. I remember one story about Aunt Alpha. She owned a small penny store. We go there sometimes for candy and soda. Her husband Uncle Wimly was a heavy drinker. He worked a small farm and took care of his family. Normally he was the most humble and meek man you ever did see. But pour some liquor in him and you see another side. One day he call himself gonna put his hands on Aunt Alpha. He was gonna beat her for something he think she done. He went to swing at her and Aunt Alpha picked him up and hung him by his bib overalls onto a big saddle hook!

He yelled, "You god damn woman, you better get me the hell down from here!"

I never learned the rest of the story so I don't know how long he stayed hanging there. I do know he didn't mess with Aunt Alpha no more!

Then there was mama. I remember one day daddy come in the house real late. Usually mama don't bother with him. This time she was different. I guess everybody has their tipping point. We all got up the next morning and went to the field like we do usual. Dusk come and me, Peter and daddy go home just the same. Mama was waiting at the door with a butcher knife in her hand! She ask daddy, "Where you been last night?"

Daddy say, "Oh woman, leave me be. I'm tired and hungry and don't need to hear you fuss."

Daddy was standing next to a stack of old tires. Mama come toward him with the butcher knife pointed his way. Daddy pick up a tire and throw it and it landed right over mama's head and fell down her body. Her arms was locked inside the tire! He called himself gonna beat on her. Peter grabbed the knife from her hands. Me and Peter jumped on daddy scratching and biting him. He wasn't gonna do nothing to mama while we was there so help me God. Mama yelled out, "You come in this house and I'm gonna kill you!" Well he know she wasn't playing. He saw a side of mama he never seen before. He was afraid to go in the house so he slept in his car all night. That was one of the few times I saw mama mad and she didn't stay mad long. The next morning he come in the house for breakfast like nothing never happened!

When we lived on Uncle Beulah's farm we lived in a house on the road. Thank God; we can see cars come by! When we lived on the white man's farms we was so far off the road we couldn't see nothing. The house be out in the middle of nowhere!

No matter where we was, mama made sure we had a full stomach while we worked all day. Sometimes mama bring potato salad, fried herring and hoe cake out to the field for us to eat. We smell the fish before mama even get to us. Mama know how to cook that herring just right. She fried them herring just hard enough for the bones to crunch and crumble when we chew them.

I learned a lot in those fields. Working on the farm, dealing with folk who really don't care nothing about us…it taught me how to survive. I knows one day I am gonna leave the south but I don't know when. I know I can't read, so I don't know what kind of work I'm gonna find, but I know if somebody hire me, I'm gonna work hard and it will be alright. I also knows I won't have to wait a whole year to get paid.

Grandma didn't have to wait either. Grandma was the only black person that worked out of the white school. Sometimes we go to meet her after she get off but we have to wait three blocks away. We couldn't go near the white school. She also worked as a domestic for almost every white person in town and she was well liked and respected. Well, respected as much as white folk respect you back then. Thinking back, I know they must respect her because they was different around Grandma.

When Grandma died, she was buried in Piney Grove Baptist church in Jackson, NC. The church was full of people. None of the white folk showed.

I remember Piney Grove. We go to church with mama and grandma. It seem like I was always fighting and in trouble so they have me go up to the mourners' bench to confess my sins. The mourners' bench was the front pew in the church. You sit there until they tell you to kneel at the bench. I remember my first time. I was about nine years old. Back then when you went to the mourners' bench, older folk want to see tears running from your eyes when you come up off your knees. If they don't see no tears, you back at the mourners' bench the next Sunday. You go back until they see tears come from your eyes. Sometimes you be sitting there for the whole service. Then when they have altar call, you stand up. When the pastor starts praying, that's when you get on your knees. When he give the benediction, you free to go. You either cried or you didn't. If you cried they believe you either repented for the bad you did or that you accepted Christ. If you cried and got home and did something bad, you be right back at the mourners' bench the next Sunday.

I was the type of child that stayed in trouble. I don't know why. I went to the mourners' bench many times. The last time I went up I started crying. I really didn't mean it but I was tired of going up there. I was almost a teenager. I feel ashamed that every time we go to church, here I am at the mourners' bench. Mama know that bench wasn't gonna make a saint out of a sinner like me.

I know right from wrong but I was young, hardheaded and I had a temper. I suppose mama thinks I probably gonna come around one day. Mama prayed for me when I couldn't pray for myself. Sometimes other folk see something in you that you don't see in yourself. I believe she just left it in the Lord's hands.

Growing up I had a speaking problem. I stuttered really bad. If I come to you and tell you something it take about ten minutes for me to say it. I was teased a lot. My friends, my brothers and sisters would tease me all the time. On the days I went to school I got teased about my stuttering as well as my learning. Because I had a short temper, I would jump on them and fight whoever was teasing me. Whatever I have in my hand I would hit them with it. One day I slapped a girl in her face for teasing me. Her mama come and talks to my mama. Mama tell her, "I believe your child should know better than tease my child. It ain't right to trouble somebody over their affliction." Mama don't let nobody challenge her about how she raising her children. Mama don't cause no trouble but she don't let nobody mess with her children! I didn't get in trouble for hitting a girl. I'm gonna fight you either way. Now I know better.

Kids mess with me and grandma tell them "Y'all know to leave Paul alone; you know he will kill you!" I yell back, "You heard what grandma say, leave me alone or I'll kill you!"

Grandma thought she had a way of stopping my stuttering. She throw a wet dish cloth in my face to interrupt the stuttering and it worked. It got to where I would stop stuttering when she did that. Mama send me to the store with a note to give to the grocer because I stuttered so bad. I guess I picked it up from my daddy. He used to stutter real bad too. I still stutter if I get excited or upset. I have to really settle down before I can get my words straight.

Grandma didn't like the fact that I had a temper but she loved me anyway. She loved all her grandchildren. She loved her daughters too. Grandma even raised another woman's child as her own. Aunt Isabel. Aunt Isabel joined the family as a baby when her mother passed away.

My grandma was married three times. Isabel's father was grandma's second husband. When Isabel's mother passed away, grandma took her in as her own. I didn't know all of grandma's husbands. I might have seen one of them but didn't know him. Mama don't have the same father as the rest of her sisters. She was born from grandma's last husband.

Mama was special. She learned a lot from Grandma. She taught all her children to be responsible, even at a young age. I can remember her bringing Big Will and Red into the fields whenever she come to help or to bring us breakfast. They was younger than me but they had to know how to work just like me. And they play just like me and Peter used to do. Mama have them on top of the cotton sack pulling them along. You couldn't leave them alone on the field because the big hawks swoop down and take them. I heard the older people talking about not leaving babies alone because the hawks would get them. I've seen a hawk come down in the yard and snatch one of mama's chickens. They would get a chicken in a heartbeat so I bet they can grab a little baby just as fast!

Big Will and Red went to school when they were old enough. They stayed in school like my sisters. They all went to Seaboard Coast Elementary. Me and Peter was the only ones to work in the fields all day and not go to school. We were the oldest boys. We were responsible for helping the family get by.

Me and Peter didn't have the chance to go to school like we wanted. We worked the fields from sun up to sun down. And just like years before, we went to school only when it rained. If it rained overnight we went to school. But to know what was going on in school was getting harder and harder for me. If the sun was shining I didn't go to school the next day. I remember staying in the third grade three years. Whether I knew anything or not they move me on to the next grade. I was too big to stay in the class with the younger children. I was still teased a lot when I went to school.

Not because the children didn't like me, but because I never knew what was going on. It wasn't a good feeling. I never fit in. And this was in the segregated school with children that looked like me.

It was even worse with the white kids. I remember standing beside the road waiting for the school bus one morning. The white children on the bus would pass by and throw cups of pee out the window and call us niggers. It wasn't easy back then but I couldn't do nothing about it. They had the upper hand on me.

One Saturday night we was walking home on a dark road. We saw a car coming. We thought it could be some white boys. We didn't know. It was so dark we couldn't see our hands in front of our faces. Where there is black boys and white boys on the same dark road at night in the south, there gonna be trouble. We run into a ditch until the car pass.

It wasn't just us. The grown folk had to swallow a lot too. As a child we were taught to say yes sir and no ma'am. So I didn't find it strange that daddy had to say yes sir and yes ma'am to the white peoples just like I had to. But they didn't say Mister or Sir to daddy when they called out to him. His name was Aron but everybody called him Earl. And the white man didn't say Mister Earl.

To this day I love my daddy. It's not his fault. He did what he had to do. He bit his tongue with the white man and he made men out of his four boys.

We had to be men at a young age. Working in the fields made you a man whether you were ready to grow up or not. When it was time to harvest crops daddy and Peter go into the woods to cut down trees for peanut poles. We had thirty acres of peanuts so we needed a thousand poles. We had to cut them with an axe and a cross-cut saw. I be on one end and Peter be on the other side of that old saw. Daddy come along shaving the limbs off the tree, marking it where we had to cut it. Then they had to dig the hole by hand with a hole digger. When daddy's hand and arm got tired Peter would have to dig. I put the pole in the hole and packed dirt around it. By the end of the year all we had was a hard year's work. When we look at all the hard work we done, daddy say, "Look at this, all this work and no money. Look at what we got." I say, "No money, no school, nothing but hard work." But I was a child. What did I know? I couldn't question my life. Someone else was in charge.

Christmas come again and only by the grace of God, daddy make a way. We go back to the fields and pick the remnants of the cotton. Daddy take it and sell it. Christmas morning we was happy! We couldn't wait until morning. We had toys! The girls had doll babies and carriages. The boys had cowboy suits, guns and holsters. We used to watch Cisco Kid, Roy Roger and Dale Evans and the Lone Ranger. We pretend to be cowboys. We get on the backs of the mules and ride them just like the cowboys we saw on television.

The antenna for the TV was on top of the house. We had to run a wire down the side of the house and bring it through the window. The wire was connected to the box on top of the TV. We got three channels back then. But that was enough. We didn't have no time for TV anyway. If we wasn't working in the fields, we was taking our crops into town.

During that time blacks was not allowed downtown after nine o'clock. If they caught us downtown they tell us, "Go home niggers or go to jail."

Even as young as we were, the only time we could go through town after nine o'clock we had to be in a car and hope it didn't break down. If Dillard Druid catch us, he take us to jail. When we go to town on Saturday we go to the drugstore and buy ice cream. I go to the front counter and tell them what kind of ice cream I want. Inside the drugstore there be white people sitting at the tables and counter. The little white kids be running all over the place. We couldn't run around with them.

After we order we have to go back in the hot sun. Not in front of the drugstore; we couldn't hang out in front of the white stores. We had to go up the street to the corner. There was a big tree that we sit under. I have to eat that strawberry ice cream fast because it would melt and drip all over me. Peter be drinking soda. Black people didn't drink coca cola. That was a rich man drink. We drank Pepsi and RC cola. That's what we could afford.

Sometimes on Saturday we come to town when the stores close and mama let us stay outside and hang out by Mr. Brown's barber shop. The white people wouldn't come up that far. I hated white people back then. They treated us real bad. Throwing pee on us, talking to us any old way, bad serving in the store, cheating us out of our money. It was hard to love our neighbor.

The only good white person I remember when I lived in North Carolina was a neighbor of Aunt Bea's. He come and work in the fields with us. He was nice as he want to be. That is, until other white folk come around. Then he acted just like the rest of them, like we didn't matter. So I guess I don't know how good he really was. I learned peoples show you who they really is.

Some Saturdays we go downtown Weldon, NC. That's where everybody went after nine o'clock. The adults go in the bar and drink beer, liquor and wine. We stay outside playing, running up and down the street. This was the black area so we were safe— hopefully.

I don't know how much it would take to get a man drunk but I knew one man that could hold his liquor: Gene Ramsey. Gene was a guy that looked like a hobo but was one of the nicest men I ever did meet. He didn't bother nobody and nobody bothered him. He was a good drunk. His clothes was torn and he smelled. Gene would recite poems and rhymes to women. As nasty looking as he was, he could get the women with these crazy raps and rhymes. To this day I remember Gene rapping to the ladies, "I'm the little one, tipping through the small parts of the vineyards. Delivering a message: God delivered Daniel. Even peeled the potato and throwed the peel away and have someone to carry his trouble to. He take his trouble to the Good Lord above and I bring myself to her. If she would allow me the opportunity to change and I don't mean change in the ocean or change across the deep blue sea, I mean the change in her."

What he was meaning I don't know. It didn't rhyme, it made no sense. What I do know is he come around rapping like that to the ladies and he wind up with a pretty woman most every time. They keep him company a while and go on their way. Wherever Gene Ramsey pass out drunk at in the night, and most time it be in a ditch, he get up, dirty clothes and all, and go to church the next morning. I don't care how drunk he was, he stumble to church. Folks help him in and seat him. After church he be fellowshipping and talking like everybody else. Gene died some years ago. I never knew if he had family. He never married. I hope he didn't die alone.

When folks started any trouble in town, the owner call the white sheriff and he come and lock them up. Daddy and Mama never went to jail because they be outside with us just laughing and talking with the other folk that didn't drink or smoke. They hung out at the same spot all the time. Everybody come out of their houses and just hang outside. Kids be running and laughing everywhere.

I loved going to Weldon. I looked forward to it. We didn't do it often but when we went I knew we was gonna have a good time. By twelve midnight everything be closed and we head back to the country.

When I was around twelve I started going to a club called The Dew Dash Inn in Garysburg. It was a juke joint. We put money in the jukebox and swing dance all night to Wilson Picket, James Brown, Elvis Pressley and Sam Cook. I couldn't read so when I put money in, I either watch what someone else picked out and I pick the same song or I get a girl to come and pick something out. Back then it was three songs for a quarter. I could make out H2 or D4 but I couldn't tell you what song went with those letters and numbers. I knew what coin to put in the jukebox. I always had a good sense about money but I didn't learn to add and subtract until many years later.

There was no age limit on drinks. As long as you had fifty cents you could buy a shot of corn liquor. We had enough money to get a soda. If I knew daddy was coming to get me I wouldn't buy nothing. But if I was going home with my brother-in-law I had it made. One day my brother-in-law bought a pint and gave me a shot. If I smelled the bottle good I'd get drunk because it was white lightening. White lightning was homemade corn liquor. It was very strong. But that night I had a shot. It didn't take much and I got drunk. I didn't throw up but I was sick to my stomach. There be grownups smoking and drinking and we be right with them smoking and drinking and dancing all night. That's when I started drinking.

There was a certain girl I danced with all the time. She was a pretty thing, that Martha Smith. Martha stayed with a woman called Nub. They lived across the street from my Aunt Teen. The club stayed open every night on the weekend. We went back to the club every night it was open! Sunday night was no different. The children who had to go to school would leave early. I had to go back to the fields on Monday morning. I didn't care. We couldn't wait for the weekend!

There was a club in Jackson we went to which was far away. Nobody had a car so we all walked. We walk about three miles which was nothing because we knew we were going to have a good time. The club was Isaac Ballmer Place. But we called it the jukebox. Mr. Ballmer say, "We don't allow wall flowers in here, so if you come in here you come in here to dance!" That's when I ask any the girls that I seen dancing, "Would you like to take this dance?" Nine times out of ten they say yes. When the club was closing we knew someone would bring us home. People back then was friendlier. Most everyone knew each other. We never had trouble getting home.

Many of the folks lived on other farms near us. Most of them worked with crooked farm owners. The last year we worked Cal Gay's farm, and we didn't clear a dime at the end of the year, daddy told mama, "I got to make a change." He had a brother named Uncle Robert Lee who lived in Baltimore, MD.

Uncle Robert Lee was working at Bethlehem Steel Company in Sparrow's Point. He talked to the people at Bethlehem Steel to see if daddy could get a job there. The man at Bethlehem Steel wanted to talk to him. Uncle Robert Lee couldn't read or write either so I don't know how he got the job. He got his niece to write daddy a letter to see when he could come to Baltimore. Daddy went back to Baltimore and that Monday morning he went to Bethlehem Steel Company. He filled out the application. It asked what grade he got up to. Daddy said he never went to school.

The man asked, "Who filled out the application?" He didn't believe daddy filled it out. He made daddy fill out another one in his office. Daddy filled it out again and he got the job. He didn't go to school to read or write but somewhere down the line he learned. He had some of the most beautiful handwriting you ever want to see. He had what we call a "mother's wit". A mother's wit is when things come natural to you.

To this day I don't know how he learned. He told me Big Momma would send him to school and he stay in the woods all day. Then he walk home with the other kids when they got out of school. He helped his niece with her homework. I don't know how he did it. He was just smart! When it came time to weigh up the cotton at night, he have it added up in his mind before my sisters could write it out. He told them what it totaled. He read the newspaper every day. I never saw him read a book other than the bible. He knew the bible from front to back. If he read a word he don't know or you say a word he don't know, he look it up in the dictionary. He never went to school but he was a smart man. Maybe that is why I like going to school so much. Maybe I want to be smart like daddy.

Daddy didn't go to the Baptist church like the rest of us. He went to the Holy Sanctified Church in Garysburg, NC. He just liked the way they performed and reacted during service. Plus he knew Mama Lillie, the Pastor of the church. What got him interested in going to the church was one day a lady rolled down the aisle in a wheel chair. She couldn't walk. They were having Holy prayer that night. Mama Lillie said, "If you believe God can heal you, come forward!" A woman got up and pushed the lady in the wheelchair down the aisle. When they finished praying and shouting that lady got up out of that wheelchair and took four steps. Daddy was crying like baby! I don't know if I ever saw daddy cry. I saw him cry the night that lady got up and walked. I can feel those tears pouring down his face like they is pouring down from my own eyes. From that day on, when daddy did go to church, he went to that holy sanctified church.

　　　We spent a year working on Uncle Beulah Stevenson's farm. After we helped him get his crops in we would work on someone else's farm. We got paid every week. That's when we started to have money. Mama was good with money. She saved what she could and we had enough to start a new life. Daddy wrote mama a letter and told her to pack everything and everybody up because he was coming to get us. We had everything packed up. Daddy and Uncle George drove a U-Haul truck down and Uncle Steve drove his Imperial. We loaded the U-Haul up to the top. Me and Peter got into the truck with daddy. Everybody else got in the navy blue Imperial with Uncle Steve. When we drove through Seaboard we was so happy. I was waving and yelling "Bye-Bye Seaboard. When you see me again it'll be a cold day in July!" Yes, that's what I said. I knew it gonna be a big turnaround for me. I knew the next day when I woke up I was gonna be in another city. Maybe my life gonna change for the better.

CHAPTER FOUR
Stand Firm

Wherefore take unto you the whole armour of God,
that ye may be able to withstand in the evil day,
and having done all, to stand.
Ephesians 6:13

I was sixteen when we left Seaboard to go to Baltimore. We moved into a row house on North Fulton Avenue in East Baltimore. The row house was just like the one in Norfolk. It was a little bigger with four bedrooms. The family was bigger now so we needed the space. Daddy had family living here so we was glad to know a few people.

It took time for us to get used to the smell of the city. In the south, everything is wide open and breezy. It smelled different on the farm. There was fresh air...scent from the honeysuckle and huckleberries filled the air. Plowed soil, garden greens and orchard fruit—that is what I remember. Some days we pick the honeysuckle and put them in a can and bring them home for mama. The whole house smell like outside.

In Baltimore, we didn't know the pollution was what we smelled every day. Exhaust from the buses and cars, fumes from the factories. We always ask, "What's that smell?" Peoples look at us like we was crazy. Yes, it took a while.

My six months in Baltimore was a living hell! I got into a lot of trouble with guys in the neighborhood. Peter too. We had to fight almost every day because we didn't dress or talk like the other boys. We stood out like a sore thumb picking cotton!

Back then in Baltimore, there was a gang of guys called the Jitterbugs. I say they was like a gang because they dressed the same and like to cause trouble. They all wore matching baseball caps, baggie jeans, long button up shirts and tennis shoes. They was always together. I didn't know nothing about the clothing style the jitterbugs was wearing. I wore bib overalls and flannel shirts just like we wore on the farm. But we not farmers anymore, we in the city now. It didn't matter, we had to wear what we had and it didn't go well with the jitterbugs.

The neighbor on one side of us had two girls and one boy. Miss Virginia, their mama, was a tall woman with beautiful long black hair. Her girls looked just like her. I remember their names; Vanessa, Tasha and Ronny. We all dance and have a good time.

We line up in the street and do the Madison. That was the dance back then. No matter what we doing or who we with, the Jitterbugs want to start some mess.

We outside dancing and clowning around—having a good time, when who show up but the Jitterbugs, hell-bent on causing trouble! When we saw them coming, we knew it was time to fight. Daddy taught us to never back down from trouble. We got to face it head on! As soon as mama seen them coming she call the police. When the jitterbugs seen the police coming they go running! The police look at them and know they was trouble! They look at us and know we was from the country!

One day, daddy didn't go to work. We was all outside playing. Here come the jitterbugs again, making a lot of noise about nothing, planning to bother us again. Daddy heard them and came out the house.

"Hey, what is you boys doing? Go on and mind your own damn business!"

Daddy was big and over six feet tall. He spoke with authority. No child I ever know talked back to him. When they saw him they must have been scared because they kept moving. There was no back talk or nothing. Funny thing is they never bothered us again. Don't matter though, we was always ready! I was always ready to fight!

The neighbor on the other side had two boys. They used to sit on the stoop in front of our house and hang out with us. They used to help us fight too. They was always out there with us whenever the Jitterbugs come looking for trouble.

One of the neighbors' was Bud. Bud got me a job selling newspapers. Every morning at five o'clock I woke up to go to my paper route. I had to catch the bus. It was only six blocks but I was always afraid of running into the jitterbugs. That's why I rode the bus. I thank God I never saw them when I was alone.

I didn't need the Jitterbugs to get into trouble. Somehow trouble followed me. I remember one day mama and daddy went to

New Jersey to visit mama's cousin Miss Helen. We stayed at home. I was outside riding a bicycle and I put a little girl on the bike with me. I didn't know it was against the law for two people to ride on a bicycle. She wanted a ride so I told her to come on. I put her on the handle bars and we rode down the alleyway. When we got to the end of the alleyway I slammed right into the passenger door of an oncoming car! The girl flew from the handle bars into the air. She didn't get hurt, a little scrape is all. A scratch was on the car where I rammed into the door so the driver called the police. When the police came they gave me a ticket for careless driving. He asked me for identification and I didn't have none. The only identification I had was a social security card and mama kept that tucked away in a folder. I told him, "Please sir I live right down the street."

"Well sign the ticket" the police office said.

"I can't read or write sir" I answered. That was the first time I can remember that I told someone that I couldn't read or write.

The police officer walked me to the house. "Does this boy live here?"

"Yes sir, that's my brother" Louise say. Louise was the oldest so she was in charge while mama and daddy was away.

"Well ma'am I need you to sign this ticket for your brother."

Louise signed the ticket and that was it.

When mama and daddy come home the next day, Louise told them what happened. They didn't say too much. The most daddy said was, "When it comes time for you to go to court, we ain't going with you. You gonna carry yourself down there yourself!"

When it was time to go to court I took the trolley car downtown. I never took the trolley before. I told the conductor where I was going and he pointed out the courthouse when we got to the stop. I learned how to get around by recognizing the letters on the street sign. I didn't know what the letters were I recognized the shape and the order. I got familiar with what street I was on by a landmark or something else. Once you learn what the courthouse in Baltimore look like, you can't miss it. It was a big huge grey building.

I carried a letter that was mailed to Mr. Aron Seaborn. My daddy name is Aron Seaborn too. He didn't use Sr., and I didn't use Jr. I didn't read the letter. I couldn't. Daddy didn't read it either. He gave it to me because it was from the county. I showed the letter to the officer in the front and asked him to point out which room I should go to.

I was scared senseless when I entered the courtroom and stood in front of the judge. It felt gloomy even though the room was filled with light coming in from the large windows. I remember those cold marble floors and long wooden benches. The judge seem larger than life sitting up at his desk. He was looking down on me. I felt so small. There were two gun-toting bailiffs; one by the entrance and one by the judge. This was the real deal. This wasn't no cowboy and Indian television show. I did not want to go to jail. The judge looked at the paperwork and looked at me.

"You sixteen?" the judge asked.

"Yes sir, I am."

"You work at Sparrow's Point?"

"No sir I don't," I answered. "That's my daddy that works at Bethlehem Steel down in Sparrow Point." By now I was wondering what was happening; why he asking me questions about Bethlehem Steel.

"I see the confusion. But I don't know how they made this big a mistake. They summoned you hear in your daddy's name. No matter. You are standing before me now. Since you just moved here and you didn't know the law about riding two on the bicycle, I'm going to dismiss this. But I want you to remember not to show up in this court again." That was one of my first happy encounters with a white man. I'm here to tell you I didn't show up in that man's courthouse again. But that wasn't the last of the trouble I seen and it weren't the last of courthouses I seen neither.

Seven days a week I sold newspapers. At that time the newspapers were twenty five cents. I get five cents a paper. I used to sell at least two hundred papers every morning. Bud sold newspapers too. Funny thing is Bud always went to school after he sold his papers. It usually took me about six hours to sell all of mines. I don't know how I have the time to go to school after the papers was sold. I didn't go to school in so long that it wasn't even something I wanted to do at this point. I wanted to earn money so I could dress the way I want. Truth be told, at this point it meant more to me to have money than to go to school. I didn't mind working that paper route because I kept change in my pocket.

I spend some of it at the Submarine Shop where Peter work. I always liked the cheese steak sub. Sometime me and some of the other guys go and just fool around on the corner while we wait for Peter to finish his shift. As long as I didn't have to go to daddy to ask for money I was alright. I didn't have to ask him or mama for a dollar after that. If I was going to the picture show on a Friday night I had my own money. I worked my paper route for the entire six months that we lived there.

After I sell papers on a Friday I ring people's doorbells and ask them if I could scrub their steps. Most of the row houses had white steps. Whenever I could, I be out there scrubbing somebody's steps. I was willing to do it. I wanted to work.

My cousin Edith tried to get me work at Johns Hopkins Hospital. Edith had been working there for years. She knew I wasn't eighteen yet but she didn't know that I couldn't read and write. I made a few excuses and never went to apply. I knew I probably won't stay in Baltimore for too long. I got into too much trouble—too many fights. I knew it wasn't for me. As it turns out I didn't stay in Baltimore long. Many years later, she got Peter a job at Johns Hopkins. Why he left, I don't really know. I know he always had a good job though.

I knew if I wasn't going to school, I had to do something. I couldn't lie around the house. Daddy won't have that. If having a paper route and scrubbing steps taught me anything, it taught me that I liked having money in my pocket.

One of our neighbors had a contracting business. One day he ask me, "You want to work a day or so?"

"Yes Sir!" I agreed and went home to tell mama I had a job. They didn't consider the paper route a job.

I was big for sixteen and the man didn't ask no questions. No one ever questioned me about my age, whether I could read or write, if I had a social security number or not. I had a social security card since I was ten years old.

"Where you get a job at?" Mama asked like she didn't believe me.
"The man live down the street give me a job mama." I had to take mama down there to meet him. Then she say it was alright for me to go with him.

The next morning the man come and picks me up in his eight passenger van. I was so happy I had a job! When we got to the job he gave me a pick axe and a shovel. I never used a pick axe but I used a hole digger down south so using a pick axe wasn't nothing! I had to dig a drain. I worked hard that day. At the end of the day the man asked, "How you doing boy?"

"I'm alright Sir." I was lying through my teeth because I was sore all over. I was hurting like you know what! I sure didn't want him to know that! Hard work didn't bother me. I worked hard on the farm so this was nothing compared to farming and preparing land. And I knew the soreness would pass. After a couple of days the man said, "I'll let you know when I need you again." So I continued my paper route and worked for him only a few more times.

I also worked for Daddy's friend Steve. He was a nice guy. Steve was the type of guy that would give you the shirt off his back. He's the man who helped move us from Seaboard to Baltimore. It seemed like he was always around doing some good. He got Peter a job at the sub shop. Peter sold submarines all day; I sold newspapers and hung wallpaper. Peter got a paycheck. I got paid pocket money.

When Steve first asked me if I wanted to help him hang wallpaper I didn't know what he was talking about. We didn't have wallpaper in Norfolk or North Carolina. I didn't know nothing about wallpaper or hanging it. It didn't take me long before I knew a lot about it. Steve taught me everything I know about painting and hanging wallpaper. I loved that job. Matter of fact, I loved doing anything I could do as long as I had a job that was paying money. I worked with him almost every day until I left for New Jersey.

Steve paid me under the table, what he call pocket money. Even though I was working every day, daddy didn't consider it a job. Even though I was helping out around the house and giving mama a few dollars, if I wasn't bringing home a real paycheck, daddy didn't see me as really working.

One day, when daddy was leaving to go to work, he said, "Whoever here without a real job when I get home, I don't want to see you!"

Now I was working three little jobs to help out. They was all pocket change jobs but I was getting paid. I know what daddy mean by saying that. Don't matter, I was doing what I could do. But when daddy say something like that, he usually mean it! He don't talk just to be talking. What I look like asking him if he was fooling?

Louise just had a baby boy and was getting ready to leave for New Jersey to be with her husband. Lucille was already living there with her husband and Louise couldn't wait to be near her twin sister again. I made plans to leave with her.

That night I got my suitcase and started packing up my little bit of stuff. Mama asked me, "Boy what you think you doing?"

"Mama" I said, "you heard daddy say, 'don't nobody without a job be here when he get home.' "

"You know he just playing child," mama say.

"I don't know if daddy playing or not but I won't be here to find out when he get home!"

I was too big for daddy to beat on me. No telling what would happen if he start to whoop me. I suppose the good Lord even then was in the midst. He probably protected me and daddy! He was watching over me then and He surely is with me now.

In Baltimore no one ever asked me if I could read to get any of the little jobs I got. I was glad because I knew I couldn't read or write. I wasn't able to fill out applications to get a real job that give you a paycheck. I really don't know how Peter got the job at the restaurant. I suppose it was God watching over him too.

I was too big to go to school during the day like the other children. I was too far behind. Mama knows that I couldn't read or write. That's why she didn't want me to leave home to go to New Jersey with Louise. Mama believe I be better off at home 'til I was able to do for myself. I knew I didn't know how to read or write too, but I wasn't going to let that stop me from leaving. I was tired of fighting every day. I was tired of not going to school, of not fitting in. I was tired of the struggle. Maybe it be different in New Jersey. Maybe God had another plan for my life. He had to.

Louise called for a taxicab. We loaded up and they carried us to the Greyhound Bus station on Fayette St. We got on the bus and headed to New Jersey.

Shortly after we get on the bus the baby had a bowel movement. I never smelled something so bad in all my life! How a little baby could make such a big stink still leaves me shaking my head when I think about it. Everybody was pulling down their windows trying to air the bus out. I was so embarrassed. Louise was so embarrassed. I don't know why. Everybody knows a baby can't help what he does.

I'll never forget how I felt when I stepped off that Greyhound in Newark, New Jersey. Strange, but I felt like I was home. Like this was the place for me. Everybody I worked with in the fields in Seaboard was already here making a life for themselves. I knew I was going to make a life for myself too. If you ever feel like you know something for sure, then you know how I was feeling. I stand there for a minute just taking it all in. I felt like my life was getting ready to change. I don't know how. I didn't know why. I just felt different.

Mama told me that later that night when everybody got in the house, daddy ask her, "Did Louise and the baby get there okay? And where Paul at?" he continued to ask.

"Earl, didn't you tell the boy not to be here when you get home?" mama asks him.

"Woman you know I was only fooling!"

"Well Paul didn't know you was fooling so he took the Greyhound to New Jersey with Louise." Mama didn't want me to leave so I know she was sad. She pray for me all the time. This much I know is true. Mama loved me. Mama kept praying for me. I believe her prayers was answered.

Peter had a full time job making submarine sandwiches all day so he could stay. Maryanne, Minnie Mae, Big Will and Red were left at the house. They were still in school so they was safe too. Me; I didn't go to school not one day in Baltimore. I couldn't read, write or barely spell my name. Would have been too far behind to try and catch up.

My brothers-in-law, Jimmie Louis and Joseph knew I couldn't read or write but they said they could help me get a job when I got to New Jersey. They did help me. I didn't go back to Baltimore for another four years. I was sixteen and couldn't read when I left. When I returned to Baltimore for the first time four years later, I still couldn't read and I still had to fight. But this time, I went back with a job, money in my pocket and I was driving a black 1958 Chevy.

CHAPTER FIVE
When I Became a Man

When I was a child, I spake as a child;
I understood as a child, I thought as a child:
but when I became a man, I put away childish things.
1 Corinthians 13:11

When I got to Montclair, New Jersey I stayed with my sister Lucille and her husband Jimmy. I slept on the couch. I didn't care. It felt like a bed to me and I didn't have to share it with nobody. I knew when I get that job Jimmy say I might get, things was going to change. Even though I left Baltimore with Louise, I prefer to stay with Lucille.

The section of Montclair where Lucille lived was called the Harlem. All the black people lived there. Harlem was a well-kept neighborhood with mostly single family houses. There were a few multi-family homes scattered in. Lucille's house was a small, grey clapboard home with one bedroom. It was tiny. It sat back on Talbot Street in between two other houses. You wouldn't know the house was there if you didn't go up the driveway.

When I come outside in the morning everybody is at work. All the children my age is in school. Not knowing how to read or write, I didn't know what to do. What can I do if I can't read or write? I was big for sixteen so I did some landscaping to help pay my way. I worked for a guy named Slick. Slick was a hustler. He did a little bit of everything to have money pass through his hand. I was glad he let me work with him. I raked leaves, cut hedges and cleaned yards all day everyday for about a year.

Lucille and Jimmy didn't charge me nothing but I gave them a few dollars every week. I never took for granted what they did for me. I knows my life was gonna be better and I thank God for Lucille and Jimmy. I made about sixty dollars a week. Everything was under the table but I was able to save some money. I lived with Lucille and Jimmy for about one year. They taught me how to write out my name while I was with them. I guess they knew I wouldn't be working for pocket change forever.

One day Jimmy Louis come home and tell me to come with him to work the next day. He said there was a job for me. Jimmy Louis worked at Community Hospital in Montclair. He was a porter. I was scared to death because I knew I didn't know how to read or write. I didn't know what to expect but I knows if he is telling me to come, then something must be planned already.

When we got to the hospital that next morning, I met Mr. Henderson and Rug. They had been working there for a long time and had some pull around there. They already knew that I couldn't read or write but they vouched for me and found a job for me.

They took me to Mrs. Scottsburg's office. Mrs. Scottsburg was the head of the hospital. She wanted to meet with me and let me know which department I was gonna work in. She said to me, "I don't normally hire anybody straight off the street, but since you came so highly recommended, I'm going to take a chance on you. I'm going to place you in the cafeteria and kitchen doing whatever is needed—you alright with that?"

All I could say was, "Yes ma'am and no ma'am."

"You do your job and we'll get along real fine." She shook my hand and I had a job. A real job with a paycheck!

I remember her to this day—the woman who gave me my first job. She was a tall heavy-set blonde. She was probably in her sixties because she retired shortly after I got there. And she was white. She was the first white person who treated me with respect. She was the first white person who gave me a chance in life to become somebody. She let me know that I was a man and she was gonna respect me like a man. Not a black man, but a man. She was the first white hand I ever shake.

Up until now all white peoples I ever knew treated me bad, like I wasn't worth nothing. In the south I saw them treat all the men in my family that way. No respect, like we was all stupid and didn't know no better. They treated us like we were invisible, like our life didn't matter to them unless we was lining their pockets. I hated them. I hated all of them. God forgive me for ever feeling that way but it's just how it was for me. Even when that judge let me off, I didn't realize then that I was given favor.

But this time, I felt a change come over me. I don't know what it was at the time, but I feel like I was washed clean. I was given a new start in life. Something inside of me was made new. If this white woman gonna give me a chance, then all white folks can't be bad. I ask God to take that hate from me so that I can love all peoples that care about me. Don't matter what color their skin is. And from that day on, I looked at white people different. I stopped hating them. I had to.

Mrs. Scottsburg used to come through the cafeteria and fix her usual salad. She asks me, "How are things working out Aron?" I answer her the same each time, "It couldn't be better!"

If ever it snowed during my shift, I clean off Mrs. Scottsburg car before she left for the day. I was so grateful for her giving me a job I didn't ever mind. Everybody knew me as Paul but she always call me Aron. Next day she comes through the cafeteria line and shout, "Thanks Aron!" I yell back, "No—thank you ma'am!" The head cook Ed, drank like a fish but he was a hell of a cook. Mrs. Scottsburg would ask Ed, "How's Aron doing Ed?" He would answer back, "Wish I had another one like him!" I tell you, anytime somebody take a chance on you, you better do your best. My best had to be better than everybody else.

The first thing I did after I got the job was call mama. "Mama I got a job!" I was excited I could barely hold it in. Mama was the happiest woman in the world when I told her I had a job at the hospital with Jimmy Louis and Joseph. She knew I would have benefits with the job at the hospital. She wanted to know that I was taking care of myself. I know she prayed every night for me to get a job knowing I couldn't read or write. But mama always prayed for her children—and I believe a special prayer for me. When I went to bed at night knowing what I had to go through the next day, I didn't know what I was going to do not knowing how to read or write. When I think of mama praying for me it makes my day. It make my trouble seem less.

Louise husband Joseph worked in the cafeteria. He trained me on the job. He took me down to the food pantry every day about a half hour before we got off. He showed me where everything was.

It didn't matter if I could read because he showed me everything that was needed in the kitchen and where to find it. We load the truck the day before. All I had to do the next day is bring up the load to the kitchen. If I had to go downstairs by myself to get the supplies off the truck, I knew what to get just by looking at the package. I knew roast beef from ham, collards from green beans. The dietician give me a slip listing everything that need to be pulled off the truck. If it was tomato or beans in a can, I would look at the spelling. I take the first and last letter of the word and match it with the picture and word on the label. If it matched what was on the slip, I know I got it right. I did this a few times a week so I got used to what I needed pretty fast. Sometimes the dietician ordered from a food company.

One day, Joseph didn't come to work. I had to go downstairs to unload the truck. As the driver unload the truck he tell me what he pulling off and I stack it up in order. I stack the boxes up so that the names on the box were lined up. That's how I know I have the correct amount of boxes and what was supposed to be in them. I sign my name, call the dietician and she sign off on it. I load the supplies into the storage room.

When it's time to fix the patient food, I have to take the cart upstairs. I have to know north from south, east from west. After my brother-n-laws taught me my letters I knew "N" stood for north and so on. If I had to go to the south wing, I look for the "S" and take it to the south wing. No one ever complained about my work.

My not knowing how to read or write never stopped me from performing my duties to the best I could. I learned how to work using the good sense the Lord gave me and the survival skills I learned on the farm. Most times I did my job better than the person who knew how to read and write. The only problem I had was if I ever wanted a promotion or a change in job I couldn't take the test. I probably could have done any job better than anyone else. I stayed in the dietary department for the eight years that I worked at Montclair Community Hospital. Why mess up a good thing?

This was my first official job where I received a paycheck. Jimmy and Joseph helped me with my handwriting so I be able to sign my own paychecks.

When I got my first paycheck and saw that I brought home less than I actually made, I wondered what was going on.

"Taxes and social security" Jimmy explains. "...and benefits too." Every two weeks I got paid seventy two dollars after taxes and other deductions. That's what I made. I couldn't read or write but I knew I was making more money working under the table than I was making at the hospital. But I had benefits and mama always say that was good.

I was happy to have a job and nothing was going to keep me from being there. One morning I had to get to work with snow up to my knees. I didn't have boots. I owned a thin winter coat. I had to walk through a blizzard about two miles to get to work. I think the only thing that kept me going was to picture where I was in North Carolina and where I was at now, this day, with a job. I wasn't letting nothing stop me from getting to work. I was too thankful to have a real job not knowing how to read or write. The cold and snow was not going to stop me from getting there! Plenty of days in the winter I get to work and my pants be frozen around my legs. I be frozen. Sometimes only the cook and me be there. Don't matter, I was getting to work! I walked to and from work for the first two years I worked there.

I got settled into my job fast. The first couple months went by fast. I liked having a real job. I was making money, sending money home to mama, feeling good, really good. After I been in my job for a few months, I bought a few new pieces of clothes just to get by. Just enough to look like the rest of the guys. I kept my bib overalls. I used them for work clothes when I landscaped. I kept that job. Sixteen and working two jobs to take care of myself.

I liked a girl named Katharene. She was in high school. She didn't know I didn't know how to read or write. She write me notes and slide them under the front door of Lucille and Jimmy's house. Lucille always read the notes to me. I tell my sister what to write back. When a Holiday come around, I have my sister go to the store with me to pick out a card. I feel like a man now. I got a job and a little girlfriend. Life was looking up for me at sixteen.

I knew I had a long way to go to be where I saw myself. This was just the beginning. I kept working and saving my money. That job at the hospital was my life! If I lost that job, what would I do? I was not doing what sixteen year old boys normally do. I was taking care of business because I knew I had to move from Lucille's house one day. I knew I wanted to be on my own, making my own way through life.

My brother-in-law was good to me. Jimmy Louis was one of the nicest guys you ever want to meet. Hard working, dependable, took care of his family. He lived out in the country in North Carolina too. He was a drinker but always had it under control. When they moved to New Jersey, he sort of let the city change him. He started to drink more. He and Lucille started to fight more. I didn't want to be around it but I have to stay here for now. I take him to the side sometime and ask him what he doing. He listened to me. I wasn't gonna let him mistreat my sister. But I liked him too much to be in the middle of them.

When I get off of work every day I walk to see Katharene. I get off of work at 3:30 and she be getting off from school about the same time. We hang out talking on the second floor screened in porch. They lived in a burgundy, lap-sided two family home. My brother-in-law's sister Moochie and her husband lived on the first floor. Big hedges lined the sidewalk coming up to the house and around the front of the house as high as the first floor windows.

Katharene was a tall, full-figured, beautiful young city woman! I was the country boy talking with a country accent. She always try to correct my talking. Her mama used to say, "Why you trying to change him?" Her mother thought a lot of me. Katharene eventually stopped trying to correct the way I talk. She was going to graduate from high school soon. She probably knew we wouldn't be together. We dated for another year or so until we broke up. Her mother was upset when we broke off. I was heartbroken. I think she was already seeing somebody else. Shortly after she finished high school, she got pregnant. We wasn't dating anymore but when she heard that I was dating one of her friends, she didn't take too well to that.

I moved from Talbot Street to Mission Street when I was seventeen and a half. I moved in with my mother's cousin Miss Helen. She had four boys and one girl that were all still living at home. I shared a room with the boys. They was from Seaboard too so it seemed like old times. They wasn't farmers like us but they did day work on the farm sometimes. Miss Helen's children went to school in Seaboard and they were going to school here in New Jersey. The boys were my age, and soon to graduate. We hung out some and drove around after I bought my first car.

I found a used 1958 black, two door Chevy Impala! At the age of eighteen I bought my first car. I had been saving since I got to New Jersey. After I found the car, I knew I had to have a license. How's I gonna get a car with no license. I put money down on the car and the man held it for me for thirty days. I had a friend that was about the same complexion, same height, and same look. I gave him my birth certificate and social security card and he went down to the motor vehicle office. He took the written and eye test. He passed both. I went back to take the driving test. The only road sign I needed to worry about was the stop sign. My brother-in-law read the license handbook to me. He told me everything I needed to know. I passed the driving test first time out! I suppose driving the tractor on the farm finally paid off! I already knew how to write my name so I signed the form and left.

I was having the car financed so I needed a cosigner. I didn't want my sister or her husband to sign for me. They had already done so much for me I couldn't ask them. I was excited. I called mama.

"Mama, I found a car but I need somebody to cosign for me." I knew daddy would have no problem. He bought a lot of cars with General Motors.

Mama say, "I'll talk to your daddy and let you know what he say". When daddy come home mama say, "Paul called today."

"How he doing?" Daddy asked her.

"He doing good but he need somebody to cosign for a car."

"A car…I ain't cosigning for that boy to get a car!"

"Now listen here Earl," mama say. "That boy done work hard all his life. He don't ask you for much—never did. Now he need help getting that car. It ain't gonna cost you nothing. Look at the money that child been sending to us!"

Mama told me daddy went to bed without saying another word but when he woke the next morning he ask, "When you want to leave for New Jersey?" This was on a Thursday. They left Friday morning to come cosign for my car. The next week I had the car. I was happy when I got the job and now I was happy that I was getting the car. Life for me was really starting to look up. I wondered what daddy thought of me now.

I worked at the hospital for eight years and never missed one day. For the first two years I continued to work my landscaping job after my shift was done at the hospital. I worked all the time. Didn't have no time for nothing else. But after I got my first car, there was no time for the second job. I wanted to drive around after work. I wanted the girls to see me driving around in my own car. Now it didn't matter if I could read or write. I had a driver's license in my wallet, money in my pocket from a real job, and I was getting the things I wanted. Even the girls!

Come the weekend, I go into Harlem. I would turn a few eyes. I kept my hair clean cut. I wear a nice pair of trousers, a pull over or turtle neck sweater, penny loafers. I kept a shiny penny in them. I was never a tennis shoe kind of person so I always had on a freshly polished pair of loafers. I'd have a few dollars in my pocket and I was a happy young man! All the girls come around me. I know a bunch of them liked me too. I had my pick.

I wasn't going with Katharene anymore. She be so jealous when she see me with someone else. Katharene would get out of school and make a point to come by my house. I be setting outside and see her come up. "What you doing out this way?"

"Oh I'm just coming around to see how you is doing" Katharene say, like she want me back.

I talk with her for awhile and walk her home. She did this for a long time but we never did get back together. Up until she died, I say Katharene had a crush on me.

Katharene didn't have an easy life. She had her first child right after high school. Her mother, Miss Flora, died shortly after Katharene had her first child. She had three more children, all with different daddies. Katharene was always involved with a no good nigger. When a man is making babies and he ain't taking care of them, what else could they be? And I don't care what color you is, that's how I felt back then.

Katharene's youngest child, a baby girl, fell out the thirteenth floor window. She died. After her mama and that baby died, she was never the same. I think about what her life would have been like if she stayed with me. What would my life been like? Her mama knew I was good for her but Katharene was running in the fast lane. After a while she didn't want to have no parts of me. I know her life would have been different if we had stayed together. It's sad. That's just how life be sometimes.

I hung out with my cousins a lot. If I wasn't working, I was with Will Henry or Bud. We always have a good time. They was Miss Helen's sons and closest to my age. On the weekends we go into Harlem. Miss Helen didn't live in Harlem. There was a few white families where she lived. Montclair wasn't a segregated town like Seaboard. White folk and black folk lived in peace next door to each other. They even went into each others houses.

When Miss Helen moved to Plainfield, NJ I went to live with Buddy Good. He was another cousin. I lived with him for about two weeks. Then I was recommended to go see this lady by the name of Miss Campbell who lived on Mission Street. I rented a room from her. I paid twenty dollars a week including boarding and food. Miss Campbell was like a mother to me. When I went out on the weekends and was gonna be late, she always ask me, "Call me and tell me when you coming in." She sound like my mama. She always had my best in mind and I respected her for that.

Miss Campbell was a widow from Jamaica. When Miss Campbell moved from Mission Street to Greenwood Avenue I moved with her. She was one of the nicest persons you want to meet. She was a good cook. I put her next to my mama when it comes to cooking. But nobody come before mama!

Some days I come home from work and Miss Campbell have rice, peas, coco bread and fish. She used to fry sweet plantains. Those were my favorite. Sometimes we have the other plantains, the ones that weren't sweet but boiled like potatoes. She have them mixed in a fish stew. Hard to describe all the food she used to make but it was good. Oh my god was it good!

Miss Campbell was a tall woman, about 5'10". She loved her Winston cigarettes and dark Jamaican rum. She was so good to me that I used to buy her cartons of cigarettes at a time. I used to buy her white Bacardi Rum and cigarettes and would just set it on the table. It wasn't Jamaican rum but she drink it anyways. If ever someone was going into North Carolina I have them pick up a couple cartons of cigarettes because they were cheaper down south. I pay less than ten dollars a carton. When I come home late I try to sneak in and she ask, "Is that you Paul?"

"Yes Miss Campbell, it's me, Paul."

I never wanted to wake her. The front door always made a creaking sound when I opened it. I call myself easing through it but she always here me. If she didn't hear me coming through the front door she hear me walking up the steps. Every stair tread I stepped on made a loud, crying sound. I even bought carpet treads for the stairs but it didn't help. She always hear me coming in. I think she waited up for me like mama used to do.

My cousin Bo Didley was looking for a room. I asked Miss Campbell about the extra room. She said it was fine; he can come stay with us. I knew he was gonna be taken care of if he there with me. She rented the room to Bo Didley. She charge him the same twenty dollars and she treated him good like she treated me. She washed our clothes and cooked our meals, just like a mother.

One thing Miss Campbell was strict about; if you had a girlfriend she only wanted to see that one girlfriend. That's the only one that could sit at her kitchen table. You weren't going to bring two and three girls through her house.

"I'm not running a motel," she warn us. And we respected that. If ever she was out of town, we acted just like we did if she was around. No sir, we wasn't gonna mess up the good thing we got going here!

Miss Campbell owned a well-kept yellow house with a big front porch. Miss Campbell lived downstairs; me and Bo Didley lived upstairs. The three of us sit on that porch on a Sunday afternoon just talking and laughing. Sometimes I bring up things that happened on the job or what went on the night before. Miss Campbell like to talk about her hanging out days. She talked in a thick Jamaican accent. When I first met her I couldn't make out what she was saying. She probably couldn't make out what I was saying either. The more we hung around each other, the better we understand each other.

When Miss Campbell got engaged to be married, me and Bo Didley used to tell her man, "Take care of our mother. We don't want no fooling around." We was serious.

Her man was real tall and thin with hair only on the sides of his head. He was a heavy smoker like Miss Campbell. He liked his little nip too. All of us smoked and drank rum and coke out on that front porch. I smoke Tarleton's. Bo Didley smoke Chesterfields.

We was like one big happy family. Miss Campbell got married to that man about six months later. He died not too long after they got married.

I never told Miss Campbell that I couldn't read or write. I don't know if she ever knew for sure. When I came to her, I was working, driving, making my own way. Why would she think I couldn't read or write? Some people have a way of knowing things whether you say something about it or not. One of the ways I knew someone couldn't read was if they gave me directions. They say turn here or turn there but never give the name of the street. I picked up on that because I used to do that too. To this day, I look for landmarks to help me figure out where I need to go. If it's my first time going there, I make note of certain things so the next time I pass through I know I'm going the right way. If I was going somewhere I have you to write down the street address. I would match whatever you wrote to what I thought it looked like on the street sign.

When my brother-in-law taught me how to write my name, he also taught me letters. I only knew what they looked like. I could sound them out but couldn't string the sounds together or make any sense of them but if I saw them on a street sign, and that matched what you wrote on the paper, I was good! I had a pretty good sense of direction too. I never drive by myself if I was going someplace I didn't know. Somebody in the car had to know how to get there and back. During my first four years in New Jersey, that's how I got by not knowing how to read or write.

I was living with Miss Campbell for about a year when I met my first wife: Martha Louise Vaxter. When I met Martha I thought she was the prettiest girl I ever did see! It was on a Saturday. A bunch of us guys were going to hang out at the Sterling House on Bloomfield Avenue. They were having a big dance. I had my 58 Chevy Impala all shined up and looking good. I had my dummy spotlights on the fender. I was lucky to get a parking spot right in front of the Sterling House. I stepped out of my Impala just as clean as I want to be. I knew I was looking good!

All of us guys went straight to the bar. We was having a good time when Clovis Vaxter walked up to the bar. With him was a group of ladies. I asked, "Who that Vaxter?" turning toward Martha. There she stand, about 6'2 with heels on. She was light brown, like a large cup of coffee with a lot of cream and sugar, well-built, short brunette wig with a bang that draped over one eye. All of the girls was looking good but this one here, let me tell you she stood out. Every guy with me said, "I'm gonna have her tonight!"

I said, "Over my dead body you will!" I was dead serious.

She danced with almost all the guys that night but she danced with me the most. I bought her a rum and coke and took it over to her. She was sitting at a table with all her cousins.

"How you traveling?" I ask her.

"I'm with my cousin." She had a real sweet voice.

"Where you going when the dance is over?"

"I don't know. What you got in mind?"

"Well, you think you like to ride with me? Wherever they going I will take you there."

So she walked outside with me. I was the only one of my friends with a car. Martha got in the car and we drove off to White Castle. The guys I come with be standing on the corner looking at me drive off with prettiest girl at the dance.

Three carloads of us ended up at White Castle, eating burgers and having a good time. I brought Martha back to Vaxter's house, said goodnight and asked her, "What you gonna be doing tomorrow?"

The next day I pull up to Vaxter's house and there she is, that same beautiful lady that stole my heart last night! I pick up Garland Stevenson and Pat and the four of us go to the drive-in theater in Newark. I wasn't even looking at the movie so I can't tell you what played that night. I was staring at Martha the whole time. I claimed her as my girlfriend that night. I was with her almost every day after that. I get off of work and pick up Martha. We go to White Castle a lot. Sometimes we go to the pizza parlor on Grove and Walnut. Sometimes I bring her around to Miss Campbell's house. Miss Campbell really like her.

Now Martha's sister Pearl—she was another story. Martha was born in Mississippi and moved to Gary Indiana. When she turned of age, she moved with her sister to Montclair. I'm so glad she did. Pearl couldn't stand me at first sight! Martha lived with her and watched her children. When I come around and pull Martha from the house, all that free babysitting stopped.

Martha and me was always together. I knew I was going to marry her. We dated for about a year when I went to the jewelry store on Bloomfield Avenue and put an engagement ring on layaway. The ring cost me about six hundred dollars. That was a nice ring back then. A week later I paid for the ring and asked Martha Vaxter to marry me. She like to have a fit! "Yes, yes, and yes!" she yelled. "I thought you was never gonna ask me!"

A few months passed and Martha and me planned to be married on October 23, 1963.

When I told Peter I was getting married, he said, "Let's have a double wedding". He called his girlfriend Bernice. She lived in Baltimore. He asked her to marry him. Bernice said yes. Peter drove to Baltimore and brought her back to Montclair.

Me and Peter did almost everything together. We grew up together. We played together. We worked on the same farm together. We left the south together and moved to Baltimore together. Then I moved to Montclair. Peter moved to Montclair about two years later. We hooked up again. We worked on the same job together for about two years. Then we had a double wedding.

I met Martha's parents about a month before we got married. That was the first time I had met them. I was nervous. Martha had already told them I asked her to marry me. She also told them I was thirty. They seemed to like me. They greeted me like they had known me all their life.

I remember Mr. Vaxter say, "So you the boy that wants to marry my daughter huh?" He had a dip of snuff in his lip.

"Yes sir, if it be all right with you?"

"Well I guess it alright, you done asked her already. Am I right?"

"Yes sir." I felt like a fool. I made one mistake already; I didn't ask him first.

Mr. Vaxter was a short, dark-skinned fella. He lost three fingers on one hand from pug-wooding in Mississippi. He talked with a deep southern accent until the day he died. I only saw him three times; this first visit, at the wedding when he gave Martha away to me and at his funeral. He died not too long after we got married. I was glad he got to walk his beautiful daughter down the aisle.

About two weeks before we got married, me and Martha went to city hall office in downtown Montclair to get our blood tests. When we got our blood tests, Martha found out how young I was. The clerk said I needed someone to cosign. So I went and got my cousin Buddy Good. He signed for me.

When I first met Martha I told her I was thirty. I hung around older guys, I was working two jobs and I was bigger than most boys my age. There was no reason for her not to believe me. Her cousin Vaxter even went along with me and told her I was thirty. I don't think it mattered much to him.

Martha was mad as the devil but she didn't change her mind. I was happy she didn't.

"If I told you my age would you been bothered with me?" I asked her. "Do it matter how old I am anyhow?"

"Well…" she says.

What could she say? We standing here in love getting ready to say "I do" to each other soon. We already made plans for the wedding. We have to call everything off if she changes her mind.

I had to hold on to what I had no matter how I had to do it. That's why I didn't tell her my real age or that I couldn't read or write. I was in love. I wasn't gonna give up my whole card.

Martha found out I couldn't read or write about a week before we got married. I had lied to her once so I had to come clean this time. The truth had to come from me and not somebody else. I remember it was just me and Martha at our favorite pizza parlor having dinner one night.

"There's something else I got to tell you since you know how old I am." I was nervous she was gonna get up and leave after I tell her my secret. I was thinking what I done got myself into now. It don't matter now because I had to come clean. If we to be together I can't hide nothing from her. So I waited for her to finish eating before I told her. Anything I ever had to tell Martha, I would wait to after we ate. I don't want to mess up nobody's appetite.

"I didn't have a chance to go to school."

"Yeah."

I think she was waiting for me to say something else so I continued, "Jimmy and Joseph taught me how to write my name so I can sign my paychecks."

"Yeah", she say again. This time she was looking right at me.

"They taught me my letters so I can get by but I can't read or write."

I wasn't sure how she was taking all this. I had to tell her because I didn't want to lie to her again. She was too sweet. You ever taste something and you didn't want the taste to leave your mouth? Well, that's how I felt about Martha. I didn't ever want her to leave.

"Yeah", she say again. "That's alright. I love you for who you are. I will help you learn how to read and write."

It was like a thousand pound bale of cotton lifted from my shoulders. I felt like a little kid in that country candy store, picking out something sweet! All the while inside me I was shouting hallelujah! The city girl probably leaves me when I say I can't read or write. But I guess God knows the best for me. He sent me a country girl who understands me. Believe me, when you ask God to do something, and you mean it, He will do it. From the age of sixteen to the age of twenty God has taken good care of me.

The night before I got married to Martha, me and Peter had a bachelor party. It was held at one of our favorite bars in Bloomfield. There was probably twenty five to thirty guys there celebrating with us. Peter and me had some of the same friends. After the bar closed we went back to Montclair and hung out at an after hour joint, just drinking and laughing all night. It was daylight when we left. We was supposed to get married in a few hours. When I got in, Miss Campbell asks me, "Boy, isn't you getting married at three o'clock?"

"Yes ma'am". I went upstairs and fell asleep. Next thing I know, Miss Campbell was knocking on my door waking me up. Me and Peter was both running late. Everybody was already at the church when me and Peter come running in. Our ladies were in the back of the church mad as hell! The wedding party was at the altar with the preacher. The usher was waving his hand signaling to them, "Here they come, here they come!" We come through the side door and walk up to the altar. The preacher whisper to us, "I was about ready to leave!"

Peter was looking clean in his black tuxedo and white shirt. We both wore black and white. Martha and Bernice both wore beautiful white dresses with veils over their faces. They walked down the aisle one at a time until the four of us were united at the altar. When I saw Martha I got butterflies. She looked so beautiful. I didn't want to mess up anything. I was excited. When I get excited I stutter. I didn't want to stutter. I was nervous and scared. But later my cousin said, "You didn't even stutter when it was time to say your vows. You just spit it right out!" It was by the grace of God that I didn't stutter through my ceremony.

Martha's father walked her down the aisle and Bernice's brother walked her down. This only the second double wedding in Montclair and everybody was there. The street was covered with people. Everybody was outside cheering us on as we drove down the street in our limo. Here I was, twenty years old, working two jobs, riding down the street in a limousine. If I ever let the thought of me not being able to read or write creep into my mind, I would not have done any of the things I was doing. I felt like I was on top of the world. I knew I was a man at the age of sixteen. I was doing a man's job at that age and before. When I left home at sixteen, all I had to do was keep on working and taking care of myself. I didn't have to ask nobody for nothing. A man thirty or forty wasn't doing what I was doing. They was asking me for money! I knew I was doing what I had to do and it felt good. Now at twenty, I felt like my life was beginning for the first time.

After the wedding, we went to our reception at a meeting hall on Maple Avenue. The food was cooked by my sisters and cousins. They decorated the hall in white and different color ribbons. Everything was set up real nice. We danced all night. My father told us, "I raised two nice sons together and I lost two nice sons together. But I gained two nice daughters!" It made me feel good when I heard daddy say this. He knew he didn't give us an education but he felt proud that he raised two good men. He gave us everything he could give us and in the end, to him, it paid off. He tell us often, "I may not gave you all what you needed, but I gave you the best I had." That was good enough for me.

This was the best time of my life. Coming from the farm to this life, I can't begin to tell you how it made me feel. I didn't know how to read or write but I was doing better than the one that spent years in school. If I had to do these four years over again, I wouldn't change a thing. What I held in for four long years wasn't easy. When you are out someone may ask you to read something and you know you can't read. That's not an easy feeling. Now I know how a gay person feel when they coming out the closet for the first time. It's a weight that stay on you until you find the courage to get it off. It's not easy. You don't know how peoples gonna take you. You don't know how coming out in the open gonna change things for you. If you never been there then you don't know how it feel. I had to fake it until I could make it and it worked. I had plenty of girlfriends in those days and no one did know about my education. Everybody thought that I had finished school because I was big, I worked and was driving. I looked the part and walked the talk. Nobody had any reason to question me.

When someone read this book, they gonna ask themselves, how did he make it and he didn't know how to read or write? I tell you, it wasn't easy. Close your eyes for a few minutes and try reading this book. Then think about me. You might know what I am talking about. It be like a blind man making his way through the world. He learn to use the other senses he got. That is what I had to do. I had to use my common sense, my mother's wit. I learned to work with my hands. I listened to folk and watch what they did. I made a point not to let my weakness get the best of me.

One day, a woman ask me, "How did you ever grow up and make it without ever knowing how to read or write?" I told her, "That's the sixty four thousand dollar question. You can't answer it but I can. I'm here doing something for you that you can't do yourself." In other words, she can read the directions, but she can't put it together. She had a bunch of educated peoples come by giving her a price to do something. I did it better and a whole lot cheaper. She had her job done best by me who can't read and she had money left in her pocket!

You know, I never blamed my parents or beat myself upside the head. They did what they had to do. They believed in hard work but they worked hard for the white man. The white man took the books, the white man took my freedom, but the white man didn't take my mind. So I forgave them. I had to get past that hate to become what I wanted to be in life. If I stayed that way, filled with hate, it be on me, not the white man. If I keep the secret of not knowing how to read or write inside me, I might have used it as a crutch all my life. When I was sixteen I'm glad my father told me not to be home. I might still be home and I probably wouldn't have made it. But here I am twenty years old and living better than many. Well, I knew I wasn't going to let not being able to read or write stop me from doing nothing I want to do. It's like the word say, "I once was blind, but now I see".

CHAPTER SIX
Unto Death do us Part

Therefore shall a man leave his father and his mother,
and shall cleave unto his wife:
and they shall be one flesh.
Genesis 2:24

After me and Martha got married, we stayed with Miss Campbell for about month. Martha and Miss Campbell got along real good. Then we found our first apartment. We moved to a little place on Bay Street. It was a four family apartment building. We lived on the second floor into a four room apartment.

The only thing we had when we moved was the clothes on our backs. No furniture, no dishes—nothing! We made a bed out of two quilts. We slept on that for about a week. We had saved a little money for furniture. First we bought a bedroom set and kitchen table and chairs. Our bedroom set was walnut. It was real nice. We got a bed, mattress, highboy, dresser and mirror, for six hundred dollars at Field's Furniture Store.

We used to have little dinner parties and have a real good time. We throw fish fries just like mama and daddy and grandma before them. Everybody in the building be there. Once we got our living room and dining room furniture we cut all that out. We didn't want nobody messing up our furniture.

We both worked so we were able to pay our bills on time and build our credit up pretty fast. I bought a brand new, 1964 black two-door Chevy Impala. I had this ordered.

Twenty one years old, a new wife, new apartment, new car, nice clothes, and did not know how to read or write. You couldn't tell me nothing—I was living the life I know I could live! I knew Peter and Bernice was happy too. I could tell just by looking at them.

The four of us had some good times together. We went to the movies together. Sometimes we just go for a walk in the park; just laughing and doing what newlyweds do. Me and Martha lived on one side of the street. Peter and Bernice lived right across the street from us. Bernice was the quiet type. She didn't like to go out. She wasn't the hang out type so Peter stayed home with her.

But that didn't stop me and Martha. We did everything together. On the weekends we go to the clubs and have a good time! We was still a young couple so we was having fun. We know one day the fun was gonna stop. We wanted a family one day. Each of us knew the responsibility of taking care of a family. I be helping to take care of mine since I was six years old.

Peter and Bernice had a baby girl before they got married. They went on to have another two girls. They need a babysitter to do what me and Martha was doing. They couldn't hang out without having to find and pay for a babysitter.

Peter had a nineteen fifty six Pontiac when he come to New Jersey. He put on the side of the car *"For Lovers Only"*. That all changed when he got married. He had to take that off his car when they got married because Bernice wasn't having that! She said she wasn't gonna ride around town with that on the side of the car. So Peter took if off. The boss had spoken! Bernice and Martha both knew their men!

Martha loved to go fishing. She could fish all day and all night. She come home with these little bitty fish. I ask her, "Woman, why you bring these little fish home? You know to throw those back!" She love to fish. Martha and Miss Oma would leave out six o'clock in the morning and not come back until nine and ten o'clock at night. If I had a problem with it, too bad!

Sometimes me and Martha go to the Apollo Theater in Harlem, NY. We saw James Brown at least twice a month. Seem like he was always performing there. We also saw Gladys Knight and the Pips, Smokey Robinson and the Miracles, The Four Tops. One night we went to the Apollo to see James Brown. When we left the Apollo a couple hours later, everybody was outside rushing about and talking about this Malcolm X dude. As we headed down 125th street, we could see the traffic start to back up. It come over the radio that Malcolm X had been shot and killed. The Harlem Tunnel was shut down! Every tunnel leading out of New York City was closed.

I wasn't familiar with Malcolm X. All I did was work. But I knew he had to be something important to close down the tunnel. When we got to the tunnel, cars were backed up pretty deep. We had to get out the car. The police checked the trunks and everybody's identification. By the time we got home it was daylight and time for Martha to go to work. I'll never forget that night.

During that time, Martha got a new job. Before that she was doing daycare out of her sister's house. It was the day after we got stuck at the Harlem tunnel that Martha was to start her new job at the factory in Cedar Grove. By the time we got home all we had a chance to do was change clothes and get to work. I carried her straight to work. I didn't have to be to work until later that day. It was my day off from the hospital but I had a second job at the filling station working second shift; 3-11. Martha caught the bus home because I couldn't pick her up. We soon realized that we needed another car. My boss Carl had a 1955 Chevy, standard shift. Martha couldn't drive a stick so I let her drive the new car so she would have transportation back and forth to work.

While I worked at the filling station, I learned how to do mechanic work just from watching my boss. I learned how to change oil, fix flat tires, and give a tune up. When you can't read you learn to make up for it in other ways. But I had a problem pumping gas. I had to learn high test from low and I had to learn fast! When people come in and ask for high test, I knew it was the higher number. If they ask for plus, I knew it was the one right next to it. And low was the lower number. Remember, I didn't have a problem with numbers.

I learned a lot at the filling station. I started buying old cars and fixing them up to resell. I used to have five or six cars in a big open lot between the house I lived in and the next. I fix up the cars and sit them on this lot with FOR SALE signs on them. I did this for about four or five years. I was buying and selling so many cars that I received a letter from the state capital stating that I would have to get dealership license if I continued. But I kept on selling— I just had to be smarter about how I did it.

One day after Martha come home from work, we was sitting at the table eating fried fish, cornbread and french fries. She ask me, "I was just thinking, you think we should try having a child?"

"I thought about it, but I want to be in shape to be able to afford a child. If you have to stop work, I want us to be able to have the same life we having now."

Martha understood what I was saying so we continued to work for about three years. We made a lot of money and saved a lot of money. Life was pretty good. About a year later, she came home and told me, "I have to go to the doctor tomorrow for a checkup. I haven't had my monthly."

When I come home from work the next day, Martha was as happy as I ever seen her!" She served me dinner as she usually do. We sitting down eating when she tell me, "I'm four months pregnant." I couldn't keep my joy down. I stopped eating, jumped up and started kissing on her. We had prepared for this day and the money was right. I knew we was gonna be alright.

Right after me and Martha celebrate her being pregnant I got the flu. I went to the family doctor. I had been going to him for about four years. He worked at the hospital but on Wednesdays he had office hours out of his home on Orange Road. The doctor was up in age, probably in his seventies. He was well known throughout the community. He was probably the best known black doctor in town. His wife was his assistant. I always liked him. He was important in the community and I liked that.

This doctor knows I am allergic to penicillin. It is in my chart. When he come toward me with a needle getting ready to stick me I asked, "Doc you know I'm allergic to penicillin, right?"

"Yes Paul, this is not penicillin." He assured me that I had nothing to worry about so I sat down on the side of the examination table.

Well, he pricked me with the needle and within no time at all I felt everything spin around and around. A strange sensation come over my body. I felt like I didn't know where or who I was, like I was in somebody else's body. I looked at the doctor and it seemed like horns was coming out the top of his head. Before I know it, I was on top of him, pounding him in the head and beating him as hard as I could.

By that time, the people in the waiting room and the wife heard some commotion coming from the room. I only know what they told me. They say I looked up with glassy eyes like a crazy man. I had my hand up in the air balled up in a fist getting ready to punch him again. I stopped mid-air and run out the office when the wife come in. He was hurt bad—laying on the floor bleeding from the face. They called the police for me and an ambulance for him. When the police seen me walking down the street, they stopped me. I didn't know where I was going but I was heading toward home. My car was still at the doctor's office. I had no idea of what just happened. I didn't know where I was going on. Next thing I know, Officer McGill was rolling up next to me.

"Seaborn, what is the problem?" McGill asked.

"There ain't a problem." I really didn't remember beating on the doctor. I was dazed.

"Well, we got to take you down to the hospital Paul."

No sooner than I got there the doctors rushed me into a room. I had broken out all over my body. They gave me something to take away whatever the penicillin did to me. I stayed there for a few hours and then they released me. It was another day before I felt like myself. Martha called my parents. They picked me up and we went back to Baltimore. They carried me to Johns Hopkins for testing. I was there for about two weeks.

When I returned to Montclair I learned that I had beaten the doctor unconscious. He was in the hospital in a coma. People started telling me what happened. I couldn't believe it. I wasn't in my right mind when it happened. I didn't even remember what had happened. A couple months later the doctor passed away. He never regained consciousness. They say it was because of his heart but some folks thought it was because of me.

I felt bad about the situation. When I come back from Baltimore, I went back and told the family I was sorry. The wife accepted my apology. She knew I had no memory of anything that happened except the doctor coming toward me with a needle. The last thing I remembered was the doctor telling me to lay down. And now he is dead. Everybody knew I had some kind of reaction. I was never arrested. They knew something happened that made me act that way. If I go by there to this day, I think about it. The doctor's old house is burnt down now.

About five weeks after that happened Martha went back for her monthly checkup. She wasn't feeling too well. "Martha, you had a miscarriage," the doctor told her. That was just like shooting her in the head. I was at work when she called the hospital and asked my boss if she could speak to me. I told my boss what happened. Miss Jamie tell me, "Aron, go home and be with your wife."

When I get home Martha was in tears. She was pretty torn up. I told her, "Baby don't even worry about it, we'll try again." Her job gave her a couple weeks off to get herself together. The first week was kind of hard but by me coming back and forth to check on her, she seemed to get better. I kept her busy. I had to keep her mind focused on other things. We went to the picture show, to the park, to the stores. It took her about five weeks before she got right.

She used to take a nip every once and awhile. When she found out she was pregnant she stopped any drinking of liquor and beer. We didn't know if that had anything to do with her losing the baby. The doctor said it didn't have nothing to do with the situation. I think it was because she wanted it so bad, but her body wasn't ready to receive it. We never knew for sure.

Martha continued to work. About a year and a half later, she got pregnant again. That wasn't successful either. She lost that baby too. My father ask me, "Boy, what is you doing? When is you gonna stop shooting blanks?"

"I'm not shooting blanks, she just can't hold them."

"If you was shooting the real deal she would hold it!"

That was daddy. He was always saying something. I just laugh it off. You come to know my daddy you laugh it off and keep on rolling too. If you didn't know him, well, you just might take it the wrong way.

I was the only one of mama and daddy's kids that did not have any children. Daddy and mama both say, "Well ain't you gonna have children before we die so we can enjoy them?"

Lucille had one child. Her twin Louise had a set of twin girls and two boys. Peter had three girls. Minnie Mae had two girls. Big Will had three girls. Red had a girl. Then Red had two boys. Daddy was happy about that. He wanted to see some boys! "All these damn girls!" Then Red married a woman that had two girls. Red always wanted a big family. Now he got one! Everybody had kids except me.

I used to say, "I'm carrying your name daddy, I want to have just as many children as you did." But God knows best. Seem like we try, but we fail. I told Martha, "We gonna keep trying, we not gonna give up." I say, "If I had given up when I couldn't read or write, we wouldn't be here. So we is gonna keep doing what we is doing and we not gonna give up."

We sitting at the table, eating supper when Martha ask me, "How you feel about going to talk to the doctor?"

"When he want to talk to us?"

"I have to call him and make an appointment."

I agreed to go. Martha made the appointment for a day I was off at the hospital. We went in to the doctors and he told us, "I don't see anything wrong with your wife to why she's not holding her pregnancy. Her body just isn't functioning to hold it for the nine months. If she relaxes, she might have an easier time but we can never be sure. What do you think about adoption?"

"We trying to have our own child" I told the doctor. I told Martha, "Just because you can't hold a child does not change my love for you. Think back, remember when I told you I couldn't read or write? You told me you love me for who I was. Now it come back to that point. You can't hold your pregnancy but I still love you. What God got planned for us, it will come to pass."

The doctor was sitting there listening to me talk to her and he told her, "Mrs. Seaborn, you got a good man. The average man might not have said that."

Then he looked at me and said, "You can't read or write?"

"No sir" I said. That was the end of the conversation. You see, at that point in my life, reading and writing wasn't important to me. I had made it through all these years without knowing how to read or write. If I had to stop to learn how to read or write, I would have to give up one of my jobs to go to school. I was trying to have a family. My income from one job wasn't gonna support us. I had to make a choice. Learn to read and write or keep doing what I was doing to support what I am trying to bring into the world. I know Martha was gonna become a housewife. I wanted to be the head man of the family. That's the way I was brought up from a child to a man; to take care of myself, my wife, and my family. I saw my mother be a housewife taking good care of her family and home. Daddy was working hard so she can do that. If I had cut one of the jobs out to go to school, I would be wondering how I was gonna make it.

When we left the doctor's office, we left with an open, clear mind. We wasn't worrying about her losing no more babies or her getting pregnant. Martha wanted a child so bad, she didn't know what to do. But after that last visit to the doctor, Martha's mind was at ease. We know we gonna keep on having a good time and not worry about having children.

We got pretty close to Peter's three girls. Me and Martha took them to Central park in Newark all the time. We bought them hot dogs and hamburgers. We always made drinks to take with us. They loved raspberry Kool-Aid! We loved those girls and they loved going to the park. I think they just like being with us.

One day I ask Martha, "How you feel if these was our three out here in the park with us? Remember me telling you I want six, seven, eight kids?" Turn out it didn't happen that way. God always know best. Remember that.

"Well, I don't know about no six or eight. I want two or three and three is the limit!" Martha was firm with how many children she wanted.

"Well you can't be the boss of everything. We ain't using nothing so whatever comes, comes and we gonna leave it at that!" I laughed even though I was serious.

She just smiled and said, "You right, whatever comes, come."

All of Martha's sisters and brothers had children. Between her family and mine, we had plenty of nieces and nephews. But we spent the most time with Peter and Bernice's girls.

Bernice passed in 2014. She died from complications related to diabetes. She and Peter had been married fifty one years. I had a long talk with her a few weeks before she passed on.

"I can imagine what you going through Bernice but I want you to get up out this house. Just walk down the street and come back. Sit on the porch. You still in the land of the living and while you here, you got to get up. You will see how you feel."

We prayed together. Before I left, she said, "Paul, I'm glad you came."

Some time before she passed, Bernice asked Peter for a new car. He wouldn't buy her one. She called me.

"Bernice, I'll take care of it."

So the next day I talk to Peter and make him see his ways. Soon Bernice had a brand new car in front of her house. Bernice say, "Paul, how you get Robert to do this?"

"Bernice I told you I was gonna take care of it!"

Peter was born Robert Lee Seaborn. Bernice was the only person to ever call him Robert. Mama didn't call him Robert. Daddy didn't call him Robert. No one called him Robert. I didn't even call him Robert. At some point I even stopped calling him Peter and started calling him Gator. I call him Gator to this day. Peter loved Bernice until she died. I did too. Bernice was my favorite sister-in-law.

By now I been working at the hospital for about eight years. I was still working at the gas station in the evening. I was still fixing cars up and selling them but I got to a point where I wanted to earn more money. I was doing good, but I was working three and four jobs to do good. I was used to making a certain amount of money and it was gonna be hard to make less. I liked having money. I liked being able to take care of Martha and get the things we both wanted to have. I took care of my home and I continued to help mama and daddy.

Every paycheck I got from the hospital, seventy two dollars every two weeks after taxes, I sent home to mama. I promised her she could count on that. I found a job parking cars at Pal's Cabin. I was making over one hundred dollars a night close to seven days a week sometimes. I didn't miss that little check from the hospital. Seem like the more I give away, the more come back to me. Sending my check home to mama made me feel like a man. Those seventy two dollars every other week helped my sister Marianne go through Business College. I made sure I sent money home so it won't be excuse for nobody not to go to college. Even though I didn't go to school I made sure my brothers and sisters was gonna get an education. Mama tell me, "You married now. Home come first. Stop sending me money." I continued to send her money even after I left the hospital. I had it to send.

Marianne didn't want for nothing. I loved all my sisters but she was my heart. Marianne was ten years younger than me and I loved her to pieces. She was the baby girl and I treated her like one. One Christmas she called me and said she wanted some baby dolls. I drove to Baltimore with a carload of toys for her. The first house I bought I put Marianne in it. Later she wanted to go to school to be a nurse. I helped put her through nursing school. Marianne looked at me like a father. Whenever I leave Baltimore to go home, she hang on to me. She never wanted me to leave. When her first and only marriage got shaky, I told her don't worry about nothing. She bought me outfits over thirty years ago that I have to this day. If you saw them they look brand new. Yes, sweet Anne. She gone now but I think about her a lot.

Martha had a cousin named Della who was married to Cheetam. Cheetam worked for Mr. Wilkerson stripping and waxing floors. I knew how much pay he was bringing home every week. He told me of a job opening and I took it. I left the hospital and started working for Montclair Floor Waxing Service, stripping and waxing floors. Cheetam taught me everything. I didn't need to know how to read or write to do this job. All I needed to know was how to run the machines. Cheetam taught me how to do that.

When I left the hospital eight years after I started, I was still making seventy two dollars every two weeks. Making the same pay for eight years don't make no kind of sense! I couldn't read but I knew my paycheck wasn't getting no bigger. My first paycheck working for Mr. Wilkerson was over two hundred dollars after taxes. That was every week! If I worked overtime, I got paid under the table. I had no benefits but I was making pretty good money. I stripped, sanded and waxed floors in offices, car dealer show rooms, beauty parlors, restaurants, homes…some of everywhere. I did that during the day and stayed at the gas station. I continued to fix and sell used cars out of the lot in my backyard. Martha was still working at the factory. We got medical insurance benefits through her job.

Between Martha and the jobs I didn't stay in touch with mama and daddy like I wanted. One day I got troubling news from home. Daddy used to drive cabs in Baltimore. He was driving a cab one night when a man jumped in and robbed him. The man pulled out a long blade and held it up to daddy's throat. Daddy grabbed the knife from his throat and the blade split his hand wide open. The guy took the money that was sticking out of daddy's shirt pocket but he didn't take daddy's life. When I heard about this, we drove down to Baltimore for the weekend to make sure daddy was alright. He was good. Nothing hold daddy down for too long. He start hacking; driving his own car as a taxi. He did that for about thirty years. When he got too old, we had to threaten the doctor to take daddy's license away. He was getting into too many accidents. His license was soon revoked. He never got behind the wheel of a car again. Daddy died about three years after that.

Mama started working outside of the house when all her children left home. She was the prep cook at Bill's Restaurant. She seasoned the food, made the salads and such. People loved her food. She worked there for twenty five years. When Lucille and Louise moved back to Baltimore, they worked right alongside mama. Lucille is still working in the diner to this day. She in her mid-seventies and she get up and open that restaurant at five o'clock every morning. She prep everything, get it ready to go and then she gone by ten. I ask her, "Lucille, when you gonna leave?" She say, "Never."

CHAPTER SEVEN
A Brother's Love

*Behold, how good and how pleasant it is for brethren
to dwell together in unity!
Psalms 133:1*

I been working for Mr. Wilkerson's Floor waxing service for about two years. Bo Didley was working for Garden State when a position opened up. I know he needed help so I went to work with him the next week. This job paid more money so I was able to work one job. I was able to quit the gas station. I worked seven days a week. Five days in town doing homes. Saturday and Sunday I go out of town to a new shopping center where I stripped and waxed the floors. So that was fine. It kept me busy and I made good money. I worked for about three years with Garden State Floor Waxing.

Before I started working for Garden State, I took a job with Acro Office Furniture Company on Bloomfield Avenue in Montclair. We refinished office furniture. Peter and me was working together again delivering furnisher. One day on the way back to the plant, I got out the truck to stop the traffic so Peter can back the truck into the dock. Everybody was cooperating until this one guy pull up in his car. He didn't want to wait for us to back the truck in. He rolled down his window, stuck his head out and yelled, "Nigger, get the hell out the road!" My boss was standing in the doorway. He heard everything that happened. My boss Jack was Jewish—a nice man. I think he understand what was going on.

The guy in the car couldn't go nowhere because the truck was blocking the way. I pulled him out of his car. Peter jumped out the truck and came toward us. That was the first time I was ever called nigger in the north, at least from a white man. I hadn't heard that word up here unless I was saying it with my own kind. It brought back bad memories and feelings that I thought was gone. I realize I still had some anger in me that I didn't get rid of when I left the south. Another white man was calling me a nigger and I didn't like the sound of it. I thought I had heard the last of that word from a white person when I left North Carolina.

We started beating on him. I snagged him on the arm with a small knife I had in my pocket. I punched him in the face until our boss yelled out, "Peter and Paul, cut that out!"

The cops come and took us uptown to police headquarters. They took the white guy too. He pressed charges against us and we pressed charges against him. We was all released. The following week we got a letter in the mail saying the charges was dropped. He was a fireman. I don't know if that had anything to do with it. I continued to work for Acro for another three years.

Around that same time Martha applied for a job at North Jersey State Training School for a supervisor's job. Martha and me still didn't have no children. I figured this job would take her mind off of it some. She was offered the job two weeks later. I knew if God blessed her with this job we was well on our way. We have money and be fully covered with all State benefits. In about two days, she got a call telling her when and where to report.

She was working the overnight shift five days a week. She rotated the weekends. On the weekends she don't have work, you could find her fishing or at the casino. I think she loved both as much as she loved me.

Martha loved her job too. She worked with retarded teenaged girls who loved her and always cried for her to bring them home with her. They were all white girls. There were only a few black children in that home. Sometimes she brought home two of the girls that lived there. They watch TV while Martha was sleeping. They just loved to come home with her. I tell her, "you know Martha; you got to stop bringing these big girls home with you and you sleeping all day. Men don't care how young these girls are and you can't be watching them in your sleep." She stopped bringing them home.

When Martha was working, I hit the streets at night. Martha loved them children, I loved to play poker and shoot dice. I bet a lot of money. That's how I made my extra money. It wasn't no pocket change either. Some weekends I walk away with a whole lot of money. I never put that in the bank. I keep it in the house. I had a shoebox in the closet that sometimes have thousands of dollars or more in it. I pocket some and then use that same money to gamble with the next week.

Sometimes I get in a struggle to get what belong to me. If the houseman sees us in a struggle, he takes charge and gets my money for me. He hear him call my bet and he have to play. That's why you never shoot dice until the house man is around. He hear and see every bet that is made.

I never minded getting into a struggle. Everybody knows I'm fair but I don't lay down quietly. When I was younger, I didn't have to struggle for my money. Everybody knew not to mess with me right off the top. They know I got a temper and that I'm not the person to back down. Peter and Paul Seaborn don't bother nobody but don't push the wrong buttons either. Peter is right there with me—all the time. Everybody know us.

Right before we went into business, Peter opened a gambling house. Peter and me used to always say, I don't know how, but we gonna make us some money. I wanted what I wanted and I was going to get it no matter what. When I started making money on my own, I was able to do what I wanted to do. I was working two, three jobs sometimes. I could dress myself the way I wanted to, drive the cars I want and win the ladies over.

When I got a certain age and saw people wear nice clothes, I wanted to dress like them. I watched James Brown, Sam Cooke, Smokey Robinson and the way they dress and I said, "When I get grown and make my own money, I'm gonna have me some nice clothes!" I meant it too. I spent a lot of money on clothes. Growing up, I knew we was poor. Now that I am grown and in the city, I see what money get; clothes, cars and women.

Martha didn't mind me gambling. I was taking care of house and home so what she gonna say? When she was off, she be in Atlantic City gambling. She play the slot machines and black jack. I went with her once. Martha lost fifteen hundred dollars playing the dollar and five dollar slot machines. Can you imagine—losing fifteen hundred dollars? That's a lot of money to blow. But we had it and I was gambling that much and more in the streets. What could I say? I actually won three hundred with her and I stopped. I walked around with a bucket of coins under my arm. Martha lost the money we went in with and the three hundred I won! We didn't have money to pay the tolls on the way home. I got to the toll booth and told the man, "Sir, I don't have no money." He gave me a slip and I mailed in a check for the toll.

Even though I didn't like Atlantic City, everybody know I loved street gambling. I was going to the illegal places; gambling houses where we played poker and black jack and alley ways where we shoot craps for a lot of money. Shooting craps was what I liked to do. I couldn't win in Atlantic City, but the streets—that be different. See, people think money is only in places like Atlantic City or Las Vegas. I'm here to tell you that you be surprised how much money passes hands in the ghetto. Everybody knows where to go. If you win one time, you come back two and three.

I made my money shooting craps. If I come out that night and something told me this is my night, I'm going to bet until I go home with something. The next week I might lose two or three thousand dollars. I always played with the money I won. I never played with my household money. Coming up I was taught that you always take care of home first. I live by that to this day.

When we gamble in my day, if an argument start, there was no gun slinging and such; a fist fight or two, maybe a knife, but no guns. When money is passing hands, there is always that possibility. In my early twenties, I was always the cool one in the bunch. Don't get me wrong, I wasn't a saint. In other words, I could get the last word in. But then, I avoided trouble where I could.

One night we were all at my house playing poker. I'm the house man so I make my bet. One of the guys called my bet. He didn't have the money on him; he had to go to the car to get his money. When it was time to turn the hands over he didn't want to believe that I beat him. He jumped up to go to his car, running off at the mouth, talking a whole lot of junk.

"I'm not paying you mother fucking nothing! If you want it you come and take it!"

No sooner than he got his last word out, I punched him hard right in the eye. He fell to the ground and I kept pounding on him. I beat him bad. His whole face was bleeding. He was yelling, "Stop hitting me...please stop hitting me!" I saw all that blood and didn't know if I had killed him or not. "Get this dude out of here!" I told my cousin. He staggered up and drove off. Peter knew the guy was hot-headed and insisted I take his shotgun home for awhile. I don't know why he gave me that gun. I was just as hot-headed!

The next day this same guy shows up at the barbershop, face swollen and bruised. The barber ask him, "What the hell happened to your face bro?"

"Four guys jumped me—black mother fuckers."

The barber knew four guys didn't jump him. He is my barber too. Talk travel fast so he already know what happened. He didn't pay him no mind.

Well, the following Saturday, I get dressed real clean. I go down to the Willow Bar, drinking and shooting the breeze. The same guy that get in my face the week before say to me, "Nigga' you try to get smart last week?"

"I'm finished with it," I told him.

He and his son was there and they called themselves gonna jump me. They was talking a whole lot of smack.

"Man, I said I was finished with that!" By now I'm getting a little bothered and hot under the collar.

He didn't want to leave well enough alone. His nephew, who I was friends with, saw that he was pulling a knife out his pocket. His nephew threw his arm up to protect me from the knife. The knife come down and cut right through his overcoat. If he didn't put his arm between us I would have been sliced. It happened that fast. See, a person like that is only good when something is in their hand. He's a coward; but when nothing in their hand, they nothing—just a bunch of smiling faces. I knew he like to sling his knife around, trying to be a big man. I promised myself and the Good Lord, "if he ever pull a knife on me, I'm gonna kill that nigger!" He and his brother had killed a guy a long time ago. They could never prove it in court that these two brothers did it. They got away with murder.

I ran out of the bar, got in my car, sped home, and got Peter's single barrel shot gun. I slipped the shell in the barrel and lay it on the front seat right next to me. I was speeding like a bat out of hell. The wheels of my '66 grey Pontiac, two-door hardtop burned some rubber that night! Truth is, if he had never had the knife, I would have never got the gun. I know I was going to kill that dude and his son. They was both gonna die that night. I was prepared to suffer the consequences. I had to keep my promise to the Lord.

Daddy used to tell us, "Always carry yourself in a respectable manner. Never look for trouble. Don't start nothing but always stand up for yourself." I learned to walk away from a lot of things. If I don't walk away, I am gonna do what I got to do. But know this; I'm not backing down from nothing no matter who is in front of me. When I was little, my back been up against the wall too many times. I'm grown now. I got to handle my business. I got to protect the life I'm trying to build. I don't need to know how to read or write to do that.

When I got back to the bar, everybody just happened to be outside. They know what's about to go down. I stepped out the car with the shot gun beside my leg. Somebody shouted, "Paul got a gun!" Peoples scattered here and there. I could see the dude and his son running alongside the cars but I couldn't catch them. They got away. God was surely in the midst because I know I was ready to kill them. Then somebody yelled, "Here come the police!" I ran to the side street jumped in my car and drove home. I hid the gun in the bushes behind my garage. The police showed up about five minutes later.

"We hear some trouble happen down at Willow's. Now where the gun at Aron…we know you got one."

"No sir, I don't have no gun."

The older cops knew me. I was a straight guy, minding my own business, working hard every day, making a difference in the community. I was a big man in the neighborhood. I had my share of wrong, but I kept it to myself—didn't bother nobody. Everybody in Montclair knew me. They knew that I was cool. The police knew that too. They didn't say another word. They left and that was the end of the story. I calmed down and went to back to business as usual. To this day, me and the man I was gonna kill are best friends. We speak often. Sometimes you just have to let people know where you coming from. You show fear, they gonna run over you. You stand up for yourself, they gonna respect you in the long run.

It used to not take a lot to get me mad. I would flip on you quick. I guess some of that was still in me and I didn't see it. I can remember me and Martha's first argument. I can't remember what it was about but I was angry as an overworked mule when I left the house and angry when I got to work. I was working at the Exxon gas station when around three in the morning I was robbed. Three guys pulled up to the pump. I was a pump attendant so I pump the gas, check your tires for air, and check the oil and fluid levels. I walked from the booth toward them and they told me they didn't need anything. So I started walking back to the office. Before I know it, a dude stuck something in my back and tells me, "Back up to the cash register and give me all the money!" I opened the register and they grabbed every last cent. Then they tell me don't turn around. I was frozen. As many brawls as I been in, I froze! I liked having the upper hand. This time I was backed up against the wall but I couldn't come out swinging. It was three against one. My daddy didn't raise no fool.

When I told Martha about the robbery, she was glad I didn't get hurt. Whatever we was arguing over didn't seem too important now. Me and Martha had good times and bad times. We didn't let that one argument stop us from showing our love. We never went to bed angry with each other. "The argument didn't start in here so why bring it in here. You bring sorrow to bed with you at night, you gonna find it in the bed with you in the morning unless you is touched by an angel."

We worked hard on our marriage. Even though I didn't know how to read or write, I knew how to take care of my family and I wasn't going to let an argument keep us from having that understanding. If we could deal with Martha going through one pregnancy and miscarriage and a year later going through another one, we can get through anything. We got through that and we come too far to stop.

Being a young man, I did some things that a young man shouldn't have done. When I was out there gambling, I was hanging out with other women, drinking, and flirting around. Martha's cousins would come and tell her they seen me out with other women. I say to her, "Who you gonna believe? Who paying these bills around here and letting you live the way you live?"

My wife Martha didn't want for nothing. She kept every dime she earned from her State Job. She put some money in our joint saving account. The rest she spent on the children and Atlantic City. I never wanted to depend on her pay to help me do what I needed to do. I never questioned her about her money. I didn't care. I was raised to provide for my family and that's what I did. And I still do that.

Martha never said nothing else about it to me. She knew though. Women always know. Never try to put nothing over on a smart woman, even if she don't let on like she know. And like I said before but I'll say it again, "I'm not proud of it." I go into a bar and the women see me coming before I get there. Everybody know me…the way I dress, the way I smile, the way I handle my business. I was young and young peoples make mistakes. I made a lot of mistakes. But to keep making them, it's on me. You be a fool to step in the same hole more time than once. I wouldn't do the same things now.

Martha was from the old school. She could take more than the average women. She was like my mother—no matter what daddy did, she wasn't going nowhere. Mama used to always say, "Time will bring you in one way or the other." Mama be like a lot of women back then. They put up with the mess and then smile when they bury they husbands. Time really does bring you in one way or another!

Martha was always on my side. She understood me. She might not have always liked everything I did but we always managed to talk things out. She always had a listening ear. I loved her for giving me a chance after she found out my secret.

After two floor waxing jobs, I had learned everything I needed to know. One day, a customer said, "Why don't you start your own business?" I come home and talked to Martha about it. We didn't know how to start so I kept working and kept thinking about what that one customer ask me. To start a business, I knew I would need floor waxing equipment and trucks. I knew that would cost money. I had a little money in the bank but I didn't want to touch it. So I continued to gamble on the weekends until me and Peter had enough to buy two trucks and some equipment. I gave Garden State notice and Peter and I started "Pete and Paul's Floor Waxing Service".

I told Martha what me and Peter had decided. I thought, "Here we go again". I thought getting married together was the end of doing everything together. Now here we are going into business together.

In about thirty days we were partners. Just think, I couldn't read or write. Now my name is on the side of a brand new truck. I am not saying that God blessed us with that money because we were playing cards gambling and shooting dice. But I did thank God back then. "Thank you God", I say. "Thank you for giving us the money to start our business; and thank you Lord for giving us enough money to buy two brand new trucks and all new equipment!"

Around thirty days after we bought our equipment and trucks, Pete and Paul's Floor waxing service was up and running. We bought green uniforms with the name of the business sewed on the front and back of the shirts.

I can remember my first day. Monday morning come; I went outside and got in my truck. My first stop was at the Caldwell diner. The owner of Garden State Floor Waxing ate there every morning. When he saw me he shook my hand. "Best of luck Paul." He didn't have no idea at the time that his customers were gonna be mine. I went on for the next two weeks with about ten to fifteen customers. Then slowly but surely, all my Garden State customers started calling for me. They liked my work and wanted to stay with me. What I'm supposed to do—give them back?

My cousin Bo Didley went to each customer's house trying to get them to go back to Garden State. I ended up with about fifty percent of Garden State customers. I didn't get any of his commercial accounts but this was a good start for me. Peter's wife Bernice scheduled all the appointments for the business. I had to approve the schedule but she went ahead and scheduled. Bernice hand wrote a list for me with each client's name, address and phone number. I knew the different streets so I could look at the sheet and tell whether you lived on Caldwell or Verona. Once I know the customer, I know where they live. If it is a new customer, she would tell me. Once I got into the neighborhood, I would ask someone to direct me to that street. That's how I find it. Some of the places even someone who could read might not find because the house was way back in the woods.

My first appointment was usually a beauty parlor. I did all my businesses between 5:00 and 9:00 in the morning. After that, I do private homes until the list was finished. It might be nine or ten o'clock at night if then, when I come home. Martha be up getting herself ready to go to work for the night so we didn't see each other much those first few years.

If I need to leave a bill, I call Bernice and ask her to spell it out. I write it down and put a dollar amount next to it. Then I leave the bill for the client and tell Bernice what I did. Bernice laid everything out for the accountant and the banking. We had endorsement stamps for the checks. I didn't have to sign them. After awhile, I knew everything by sight; everything that had to do with the floor waxing business. I bought the supplies. I knew what I needed and I would tell the man what I needed. Just like when I was on the farm when mama send me to the store.

Just to think about where I come from—the cotton patch of North Carolina working for nothing. From Baltimore to New Jersey working all kinds of jobs in between, and here I am now running my own business. The Lord has been good to me. He led me when I didn't know where I was going and brought me back home safe and sound. It's no telling what God will do.

Martha was still working at North Jersey Training School. She helped when she had days off. If Bernice had something to do, Martha always fill in. Peter was still working with the city of Montclair as a garbage collector. One morning while out loading the truck, Peter put a piece of board in the hopper. When the hopper turned, it spit that piece of wood out and hit him on the back of the head. He was out of work for three months. Then he went out on workman's comp and worked when he could.

I worked by myself for about a year when we first started. Peter was working on the weekends only. Early on, I was doing about one hundred houses. I was stripping, washing and waxing floors. When we got the contract for the new stores we were set! When it was time to go after the bids, we just go to the office and tell them what we would do the job for. I told Martha how many men it would take, how much equipment and supplies, time and profit and then I double it. She would figure it out and that's what I bid. I was happy with the amount I was making, so it didn't matter to me if I was under bidding. I had a lot of jobs kicked my way because of that. I had an accountant, an attorney and a secretary. That's all I needed. I got rid of the attorney until later. Most of my customers paid in cash.

Things were looking really good for us. We had to hire men to come work for us. I was able to trade my sixty four Chevy in and got a sixty eight Buick Electra 225 red convertible. Pete bought a new canary yellow Pontiac convertible. Business was good! Me and Martha was able to save a lot of money. I was making more money than I ever thought I could make. I owe that to Cheetam for teaching me everything I know about floor waxing. He didn't know how to read either. Maybe that's why we got along real well. Sometimes I know it feel like he is all alone. I know, I been there. I was able to keep my head up because people helped me when I needed help. When you can walk in somebody else's shoes, it's easy to see what they going through. I don't know if my customers ever knew I couldn't read. I don't think they cared.

At least ninety five percent of my customers was white. Word of mouth spread and we never had to do any advertising. One customer tell somebody and they call for us to do their house. We was winning more and more bids for commercial work. We got to be pretty big in the community. Organizations would come to us for financial support and we donate. We never turned down any of the groups that asked. I was never involved in any of the organizations but I always gave.

Just to see my name on the side of the truck made me feel like I was sitting on the top of the world! Who would have known that my name would be on the side of a truck? I'm out here handling my business doing what people went to college to do. If anyone had told me this is where I'd be in my thirties I would have not believed them. This is why to this day I thank God for Mrs. Scottsburg. She opened the door for me to believe that I could have something. I will never ever forget her.

One day, me and Martha decided we want to buy a house. We worked hard every day for about a year and saved more money. I didn't want to be house poor. I always wanted to have money to fall back on. Then one day Urban Renewal come through our area to build townhouses. Every home on my side of the street was to be knocked down for these townhouses. Everyone was given the opportunity to move back in to the townhouses once they was built. Anyone that want to buy, they was matching you dollar for dollar to purchase your own or giving you money to relocate. Out of the thirty people that were forced out of their homes, me and Martha was the only ones that found a house and let them match the amount. I had five thousand dollars and they had to match it. When the townhouses was finished, we had first chance to move back in but we turned it down. We bought our first house, a two family house on Willowdale Ave. Just look at what God can do. When a sixteen year old boy move to Baltimore not knowing how to read or write and here I am running my own business, driving new cars, and now in my own home! God is good, that's all I can say.

Martha was happy. That was her first house too. When Peter and Bernice found out that we had bought a house, they went and bought one too. I guess mama and daddy knew ahead of time naming us after two of the disciples because we was always side by side. We had our ups and downs but we didn't let that get in our way from being brothers.

One day, we sat down and had a brotherly talk. We decided to go our separate ways. Peter didn't want to do private homes anymore and I didn't want to be on the road doing commercial properties anymore. The driving was getting to be too much. Some days I drive eight hundred miles for jobs. Don't know the signs on the highway anymore than I can read the street signs but by the grace of God me and my men get home safe every time. So we decided it was a good time for us to split. There wasn't no arguing or nothing. We loved each other. Right until this day, we carry the same bond.

CHAPTER EIGHT
A Change Gonna Come

Every good gift and every perfect gift is from above,
and cometh down from the Father of lights,
with whom is no variableness,
neither shadow of turning.
James1:17

The name of my business is now Paul's Floor Waxing Service. God has been good to me and Martha. He has given us everything that we asked for. One thing was missing. We knew we couldn't do nothing about it. I know I didn't come this far on my own. We asked God to lead us on the right path.

So He led me and Martha to the doctor's office. We talked with the doctor about adoption. He recommended that we go to an adoption agency. Martha called for an appointment. We went in and talked to them. Of course we were put on a waiting list. It was two years later that we got a child. It seemed like forever. But I didn't come this far overnight. I didn't mind waiting because I knew it be worth it. Mama always says, "Good things come to those that wait." So we waited.

One day, the adoption agency called us and said they wanted to talk to us. At that time, they were bringing Korean babies over for adoption. They asked if we wanted a set of Korean twins, a boy and a girl. We said yes. Then they asked us how would the neighbors feel about children of a different race? We told them we didn't care how they feel. Those will be our babies. We didn't care about color. If it was black or white, we didn't care. We just wanted children to love. We was ready.

So as time went by, we were still waiting and praying. If ever I wanted God to do something for me, He always did it. All my life I couldn't read or write so I asked God for direction and he led me. Martha and me wanted a child so bad. The Lord knew this. He never failed me yet. I know we was gonna have a family one day. I knew this in my soul. We just had to be patient.

While Martha was fixing to go to work one evening, the adoption agency called. Martha wasn't off that day but she was so happy they called she took the night off. They wanted us to come in to look at the babies that were coming over in the next few months. We thought we were going to be looking at Korean twin babies.

Martha couldn't wait until I got home to tell me that the agency had called for us to come in to see the babies. Turns out it wasn't the Korean babies they wanted us to see. A young black girl had a baby and brought her in to the adoption agency's office. We made an appointment to go to see her. They had a picture of the seven month old girl. Martha looked at the picture once and said, "She's the one!" The minute she saw this little baby she knew it was hers. It was exactly what she had asked God for—a baby girl that looked like us. She didn't want to wait for the Korean babies. We weren't taking any chances. Mama say, "He may not come when you want Him but He is always right on time". Not only was this little baby right on time, she was just right!

The agency got all of our paperwork together. Two weeks passed and we picked up little Zenas Marie Seaborn.

The lady who worked at the agency was white. She had seven children of her own. Every night she takes Zenas home with her. Zenas got attached to her. The day we picked her up, the woman's children was scratching and biting me, crying, "Don't take Zenas!" It was sad.

Zenas seem to know white people from black people. On our way home she was crying non-stop. I asked Martha, "What we gonna do tonight with her hollering like this?" On the way home we stopped at a shopping mall and picked up a baby swing. When she got home she was still crying. I put her in the swing. She still cried. When I go to pick her up, she cry even harder. But when Martha picked her up she didn't cry at all. At first I thought it might have been me. But any person who was dark skinned like me she did the same thing. Martha was very light skinned, like the adoption agency mother that took her home every night. That was my conclusion. So I said to Martha, "She know black from white." If I was ever going to hold her, I had to find a way to solve this problem.

At night I lay Zenas on my chest and she fall asleep. When she wakes up, I be the first face she see when she open her eyes. I did that for two weeks. After awhile, if Martha was holding her, she come right to me. I had to think of something. I had to go to work so I could pay the bills. The adoption was twenty five thousand dollars so you know I had to go to work. We had the money in the bank but we decided to pay it monthly so that they didn't know we had that kind of money. We paid half down and took care of the rest monthly. We didn't care how much it cost. Zenas had a home. We were happy. The Lord had answered our prayers. I had a white customer that paid one hundred and twenty five thousand dollars for a little black baby boy. Her neighbors didn't think too highly of it either. I hope things worked out for them.

Starting from the day we picked Zenas up, we were on probation for a year. People from the agency come by at least once a month to check on her living arrangements. If we went out of town, they needed to know. We couldn't pee without them knowing. At the end of the year, she was officially ours. We were happy that the Lord had blessed us with a baby we could call our own.

About seven months later, we found out the Korean twins was on their way over. The babies were here. We went to talk to them about the set of twins we wanted. They wouldn't let us have them. I showed them that I could afford them. We had a home with an extra bedroom. We had everything we would need. God had been good to us.

Look at me, a boy that grew up in the red dirt farms of North Carolina. Now I am a married man, making my own money. I couldn't read or write, but God allowed me to help some child that needed help. Zenas was the love of me and Martha's life. I tell her that today. "You is a chosen baby." We saw her and said, "You is our baby and you is special." When I come home from work and come through the door, she smiling at me. That's what I been waiting to see.

Around six weeks later I come home from work like I usually do. I noticed Martha's car is still sitting in the driveway. I didn't think too much about it because sometime she go in early with Rivers, the upstairs tenant. They both work for New Jersey Training School. Well Martha was standing in the kitchen just a smiling from cheek to cheek. She was lit up like a Christmas tree. I asked her, "What you all smiling about?" She sat down and asked me to sit down. I didn't know what she was gonna tell me. She liked to gamble so I thought she was going to tell me she hit the jackpot!

"The doctor told me I am six weeks pregnant".

"What!" I said. I got nervous. We already gone through two miscarriages. But I thought, okay Lord, you blessed me once with a good wife. And you blessed me twice with Zenas. And now you is blessing me a third time with another baby. All I could think is that the Lord keep blessing me. Then I thought about what the doctor told us. "If she gets relaxed, she'll probably have a better time holding a baby." Now that she has Zenas, she is relaxed.

"Do you want to take a leave of absence from the job?"

"No Paul, I just want to take care of these babies."

Well, she had no problem with the pregnancy. Thirty six weeks later she give birth to a thirteen pound baby boy. We named him Adrian. When I got off work, the nurse call me and asked me to come to the hospital to feed him. I never got used to holding the baby bottle at night. He was so big that he was almost holding his own bottle straight out the womb! I guess he take after his mama. Martha was a big woman too. She was six feet one.

I remember someone telling me a story about Martha in a bar one night. This was before I knew her. Remember, she is a few years older than me. Something jumped off between Martha and some dude. They say they don't know what happened, but next thing they know, Martha done hit this man and he went flying over the table! I remember saying, "Well I wouldn't like to have her for no wife!" Here I am married to the woman now! I best not make her mad.

When they put the baby to bed, Adrian cry so loud they had to put him in a room by himself. The Lord has been good to us. He blessed us with two healthy children.

A few years passed. Everything was going well. We were all having a good time. Zenas and Adrian were in school getting good grades in some classes and not so good in other classes. I took them to a tutor. Paulie stuttered like I did as a child so he needed help with speaking and reading. They both needed help with math. Martha was too busy during the day to help with homework so we figured we hire someone to help them out. We had the money. We figured the tutors know more than us anyway. They certainly know more than me! How I'm gonna help them when I can't read or write. It was enough that I go to church every Sunday and can't read the bible. I always thought nobody know.

One Sunday morning we went to church. Martha was going along like usual. Me and Martha did the devotional that Sunday morning. After we got off our hands and knees and went back to our seat, she told me she had a slight headache. I didn't think much about it. By the time service was over with, she was in a lot of pain. One of the nurses at church told me to take her to the hospital to get her checked out. I started to get nervous because I could see that she was in a lot of pain. Her eyes were real glassy and she lay with her head on the back of the seat car all the way to hospital. When we got to St. Barnabas Hospital, they admitted her. I was in the waiting room when the doctor came out and said, "Mr. Seaborn, your wife has a brain tumor and an aneurysm. It is very dangerous." They had to wait three days before they could operate. They had to wait for the pressure to go down. Martha was blind by then because of the pressure. For some strange reason, I wasn't nervous. I knew all we had been through, God was going to bring us through this. The morning of surgery, she say to me "I'm going to be alright." When they brought her to the ICU and I saw her head covered in white bandages. I said, "Lord you say unto death do us part." I knew God was going to heal her and he did. She stayed in the hospital for three weeks.

Before Martha took sick, she showed me how to schedule my customer's next appointment. She got the calendar. Where she have them listed on the calendar I count the weeks. If I serviced them on the first Wednesday, I count down two rows until I got to the Wednesday in that row. I circle the date. Then I know that is the date I go again. By then I had learned most of my customers schedules, where they lived, what services they needed. I memorized all of it. I couldn't read but I could write a little bit. I learned a lot from Martha before her sickness. I kept the business going until she got better and returned home.

CHAPTER NINE
Seek Ye First the Kingdom Of God

Create in me a clean heart, O God;
and renew a right spirit within me.
Psalms 51:10

Martha was glad to get back to work. One day when I got home from work Martha says, "Mr. Earl called. He got laid off from his job at Bethlehem Steel. He want to know if you have enough work for him to do."

Martha never called daddy anything other than Mr. Earl. Martha and my daddy was real close. He always said she was his favorite daughter-in-law. He loved the way she fixed collard greens. Every time he come to New Jersey he tell her, "Have me a pot of collard greens." She have them waiting for him!

I called daddy and told him "Yes sir, I got plenty of work for you."

I never thought that my daddy would be working for me. All my life he told me what to do. Now I am telling him what to do. It wasn't hard for me to tell him what to do either. I had grown up listening at him teach me how to do things his way. Now I'm showing him how to do things my way. He had to work like the boss tell him. I'm the boss now. When I think back all them days not knowing how to read or write, now I have my own business and my daddy is working for me. It made me feel real good.

Daddy didn't ask me how I was doing in my business. We was busy every day. He didn't have to ask. He worked for me about three months. Then his job called him back. He said, "I hope I never get laid off again. You worked me too hard!" The work I did every day was like reading and writing to me. I knew what I was doing. And I enjoyed being my own man.

Business was going well. I never had any problems with customers paying or nothing. My customers trusted me. They give me their house keys. Some of my customers gave me their alarm codes. I didn't think I could ever do anything that would lose the trust they had in me. I used to hang at the beach with some of my customers.

Back in the early seventies, upper Montclair was where the rich white folk lived at. There were a few black doctors and lawyers that lived there. The houses were huge. One of the houses that I worked at was next to Daddy Grace's home. It was a large house that had an elevator. When you come through the front door there was a huge foyer with a long mahogany bench. The floors were in good shape and I had to take care of them. I waxed the floors once a month. I used yellow butcher paste wax—different colors for different floors. I kept them up real nice.

I had the privilege of going through the whole house. The basement was like a bunker with thick concrete walls. Some of the houses sat so high on the hill you see New York City from the front room window. Another one of my customers was Frankie Valle out in Roseland. I used to clean his kitchen floor. I didn't know who he was. I was cleaning the floors of his neighbor when she asked me, "Do you know who that is?"

"No ma'am, I don't." I didn't pretend. I really didn't know.

"Well you are cleaning Frankie Valle's floors."

I will never forget that. Years later I waxed Herschel Walker's floors. Another client was a boxer who loved snakes. After Peter got out of the business and opened his pet store, this guy used to buy a lot of snakes from him. Yes, I had some pretty famous clients on my route.

I never envied my customers because I was doing well for myself. I didn't live in a big house like theirs, but I had a nice one. I was able to pay the bills. Martha was able to buy whatever furniture she wanted. But Martha didn't care about those things. I bought most of the furniture. I bought a lot of her clothes too. Martha ask me, "Paul, why you buying me all this stuff?"

Martha liked to keep her hair done. But give her a fishing pole, a pair of jeans and sneakers and she was happy. I have to dress down when I go out with Martha because peoples think I was spending all our money on me! I liked gold jewelry and flashy suits. I wanted her to always be dressed up like the way I met her. But she wasn't having it. So I dress up when I wasn't with her and dress down when I was.

When I wasn't waxing floors in those big houses, I was buffing and waxing commercial buildings. One day I was waxing floors in a private club of one of my customers. I been working for this client three years. There was always three or four people there whenever I did the floors. I always wondered what they did because they all be well dressed, smoking cigars, sitting around the table talking in their Italian accents. I always assumed they were in the mafia. Then one day I thought, "These guys got to be in the mob." Whenever I ring the bell someone be inside to let me in. I do what I got to do and yell out, "All done!" My money be waiting in the office in an envelope.

One day one of the younger guys in the group come up to me and ask me, "Hey Paul, how would you like to handle some nice stuff?" I knew what he was talking about. He wanted me to start dealing drugs. I told him, "Let me think about it. I'll let you know when the next time I come back." I took my bucket from the door and left.

I begin to think about what this guy asked me. I could see the amount of money I could make. I knew people that was dealing in "nice stuff". I knew the money they was making. I know my brother was selling. I knew he was doing real well selling. He owned an after hour joint and at the time he was still working the floor waxing business. I knew how much money I was making so I knew how much he was making. He didn't need the money. I didn't need the money. Before paying my guys for weekend work, I was making a whole lot of money. I paid my guys by the job and there was never a shortage of jobs or men to work them. At the height of my business I was using about twenty five guys off and on including the weekend. I paid them the same way I was paid when I worked for Garden State and Montclair Floor Waxing. Anything over forty hours I was paid under the table. That's how I paid my men. Much of what I did as an adult I learned from somebody, not in books. After paying my men and my taxes, I was clearing more money than any of the white men we ever worked for on the farm!

I didn't think much about what it really meant to sell drugs. I didn't think about who it would affect or where it might get me. I just liked having money. And even though I was making more money than I could ever imagine, I knew I would like making more. When you make that kind of money, always wearing nice clothes and jewelry, driving nice cars—you look important. I liked looking important. I liked being the big man.

The next month when I went back I said "I thought about it. I'm going to take a chance on it. But I don't have that kind of money on me."

"No big deal...I trust you. What you want?"

I told him what I wanted; three pounds of marijuana, two blocks of cocaine, uppers and downers. I smoked pot and drank liquor. I never dealt in or used cocaine or pills but I knew what to ask for.

He gave it to me—all of that. He just handed it over. It was that easy. That is the day I became a drug dealer. I got rid of my first shipment in less than two weeks. I went on to sell drugs for another eight years. I was able to save more money than I made in my business. That doesn't include the money I spent. I spent about that same amount on clothes, cars, women, and liquor. If Martha wanted to go some place, I sent her. I helped a lot of people out with some of that money.

Selling drugs was the biggest mistake of my life. I'm not going to say all of it was a mistake because I know what I was doing. I liked having money. I liked being able to get whatever I wanted, even though I was able to that with the income from my business. I was looking at the dollar bill at that time. The more dollars pass through my hand, the better I felt. A whole lot of dollars was passing through my hand at any given time. No matter how much money I had I saw a way of making more. It made me feel very important. I liked feeling important. I was "the man" in Montclair.

A friend of mine used to cut my cocaine. I watched him do it a few times then I started cutting it myself. The cut is usually two thirds of the cocaine. That is how you increase the amount. That is how you increase the profit. You might start out with a few thousand dollars worth of cocaine and end up with ten times the amount after the cut added in.

When you cut cocaine you have to snort some to see how strong it is. When I started to cut my own, I started to snort it to test it out. That's when I started using cocaine. So now I was not only selling it, I was using it.

Martha didn't know I was using cocaine. She knew I smoked a little reefer. I was always real cool. If I told you I was using, you would never know it. Alcohol was another story. I had a problem with alcohol. I started a lot of fights when I drank. I didn't know how to control my liquor. I could control the drugs but liquor—no. But I didn't let that stop me. I kept drinking. It never interfered with my job. It never caused fights with Martha. It never got in the way of me as a father. I can't say they never saw me drunk but they never saw me sloppy drunk. You never know what your children are watching so always pay attention to it. If you got kids, and you is doing something wrong, they is watching and it gonna sneak out somewhere. When Zenas became a woman, she told me, "I remember you smoking that reefer." I didn't know she was watching but she was. Be careful what you do and say around your children. They gonna pick it up, good or bad.

A country boy growing up in the city; never had nothing but everything I touched turned to gold. I was gonna keep going with the flow. Nobody was going to tell me what to do, how to do it or when to stop. I had already stopped listening to God. Even though everything I had, it was by the grace of God. But with me taking this turn into drugs, I knew it wasn't God. I knew God had nothing to do with it and I really didn't care. I saw something I could do to make a lot more money and I ran with it.

Sometimes you get too big for your pants. You make moves that you shouldn't but you keep going. After I turned over that first shipment and saw the kind of money I could make, I didn't even think about God no more. I only thought about myself and the buck that was being turned over. It didn't matter that I was messing with the mob. I was paying them. I didn't owe them nothing and they didn't look to me for nothing. As long as I didn't owe them, they didn't own me. That was my plan. That's how I kept it.

I wasn't going to listen to no one else anyhow. All I could see was money, money and more money. Money bought me nice suits—seventy five to one hundred suits at one point. I wore big gold chains with eagles. I was flying. I had a gold coin on a chain hanging from my neck just because. If that wasn't enough I had a gold cross made with diamonds and rubies. That hung from my neck too. I wanted to believe the cross was protecting me. I had women hanging from my neck too. I was a married man, a father, a son. Some of the stuff I was doing I wish I didn't do. I done some things I ain't too proud of but I'm telling you my story and this is part of it. And it don't end here.

One day, I decided to open up a night club called the Top of the World. A man owned a building with a bar on the main floor and an empty space above it. He had a for rent sign in the window.

"Hey man, how you feel if I open a night club upstairs?"

"Alright" he say.

"Now I don't have a liquor license. Can I order my liquor through you?"

"Alright" he say.

So I went out and bought the bar furniture and light system. I knew a DJ called Pretty Black. He started working for me. I got a few women to serve and wait tables. Martha was by my side for the grand opening. There were so many people lined up to get inside I couldn't fit everybody in.

I was well known in town. I had a successful business. I dressed well. I looked the part. But I continued to sell dope, even though I was making more money than I could have ever thought I would ever make. I knew I was going to make money. I didn't know how, I didn't know when, but when I look back over my life I know it was all in God's plan for my life.

Martha suggested that we do something for the kids after she saw all the support we were getting for the nightclub. We threw a dance for the kids. No alcohol. We gave prizes to the best dressed. We had a club full of small children just having fun, eating cake and ice cream. Every year we did something as a business to keep our face in the community. We supported a lot of different organizations.

I ran the night club for about three years. I was still involved in drugs big time. During the day I was in green uniform with my name on it. At the mid week, I was in leisure suits. On the weekend, I wore three piece suits, tie, and pocket square, Stacey Adam alligators— the whole nine yards. I was sharp as a tack! That was every weekend. Still, no one knew the secret I was carrying around. I was dealing drugs, running two successful businesses, contributing to my community and still I couldn't read or write. But I knew how to make money. If you know how to read and write and try to cheat me, you be barking up the wrong tree! I may not know how to read but I know how to count money. When I tell you about all this, nice clothes, jewelry, cars, women—I am not bragging, I am just telling you like it was. It was my biggest regret in life.

The Montclair police wanted one of us: me or Peter. They knew what we was doing. We had pull with some of the older cops in the force. All they cared about was getting their palms greased. They didn't bother us. Then they started retiring. One by one, the police with the greasy palms left. When a new group of cops come on, I guess we became targets.

One Friday night after I had just picked up my shipment the Montclair Police raided my house. I had been home a few hours. I had already carried my stash to the basement where I kept it. I put the wrapped cocaine in the packages of freezer meat. The uppers and downers were kept in empty vitamin containers. I hid a half pound of marijuana in my bedroom. That was my personal stash.

When the cops rang my doorbell I went to answer it because I was expecting some folks for poker that night.

"Who's there?" I yelled out.

No one answered so I looked out the diamond shaped window in the door. I didn't see nobody so I opened the door. I thought the guys was trying to be funny. When I opened the door at least five police jumped on top of me.

"Paul Seaborn, this is a raid! You are under arrest for possession and attempt to distribute!"

I go along with them. I'm not going to bow down and say, "You got me." No, I say, "What is going on?" I had to appear like I didn't know what they was talking about.

They come through my house like a storm blowing through a corn field, throwing furniture around, pulling the smoked mirrors off my wall, searching everywhere they could. I'll never forget this one red-haired cop. He was nasty. He was the main one that wanted to tear up my house. They took all the pillows off and searched inside them. Turned over the furniture; pulled out all the drawers; turned out everything. This little red-haired cop didn't want to stop. He pulled the meat out the freezer. I didn't say nothing! He had twenty thousand dollars worth of cocaine in his hand, and he put it back. That's when I said, "Look man, I got half a pound of marijuana and six hundred dollars. That's all I have!"

I didn't want them to check nothing else or to tear up my house anymore. Martha was gonna be mad as the devil as it was. She was at work. Lucky for me the children were at Miss Ruby's house. When Martha come home, Peter had already bailed me out of jail. I told her what happened. She was pissed off! I wasn't gonna argue with her either because she had every right to be mad. The house was torn up, I had gone to jail, and put my family in jeopardy. They also tried to charge Martha with possession and attempt to sell. She didn't have nothing to do with the wrong I was doing. Martha didn't deserve to be caught up in this mess. This trouble here because of my greed and wrongdoing. I didn't want to lose Martha or bring harm to my family. I never meant for any of this to happen but it did. I got to deal with the consequences. I know a change was gonna come. Good or bad, it had to.

I went to trial and was found guilty. I had to wait about six weeks for my sentence. While I waited, I got my house in order. I hired an attorney for Martha and one for me. Once I got Martha off, I had to fight for myself. The judge told me I was looking at thirty five years. When my lawyer come out, he told me, "We going to postpone this and put in for another judge." He know he could get me out of it. "I can get you out of the thirty five years. I don't think you'll have to do more than a year." Here I was looking at thirty five years and I only had to serve one hundred eighty days out of the year sentence my lawyer thought I would get!

The courthouse was full of my white customers who all vouched for me. My father spoke first. Then one customer spoke for all the customers. The judge said, "Mr. Seaborn has broken the law and he must serve his time. He will be home for Christmas."

The day that I went to trial to be sentenced, that was the last day I saw my children until I was released. Immediately after my sentence I went to jail. I gave Martha everything that was on me—my watch, gold bracelets, my wallet, all my rings except my wedding band. I had fifteen hundred dollars in my wallet. I was sick that I let this happen. God had blessed me with so much, not being able to read and write. He blessed me with enough money to spend two lifetimes over and I wanted more. I hope Martha was gonna stand behind me like she did when I told her I couldn't read or write.

The police handcuffed me and walked me out the courthouse. As I was walking from the courtroom, I looked back. Martha, mama, daddy, Minnie Mae was all crying. I knew it had to be this way. I did the crime now I had to do the time. I didn't like it but it has to be this way. I was sick over all of it. I could hear my grandma's words playing back and forth in my mind. "All you can't pull; you get behind and push it." My grandma used to say that to my Uncle Jack when he went back and forth to jail. I understand what she mean now.

The sheriffs carried me to a small room where I was given a green jumpsuit. I was wearing a three piece dark gray suit with a burgundy tie and pocket square, and a pair of black leather Stacy Adams. I felt sick to my stomach. One hundred eighty days could have been one hundred eighty years the way I felt. My whole insides turned upside down. Thinking about where I was gonna be for the next six months left an ache in my gut like someone had punched me over and over again. After I changed clothes, I was taken to a cell that I was sharing with two other men.

It was about one week before I was transferred from Newark to West Caldwell Correctional Center. I was shackled around my ankles with a chain that run up to my waist and around the waist to the back where my hands were cuffed behind me. When I arrived, they put me in a holding cell until I got my floor assignment. I was glad to get out of that little cell. It felt like the walls was closing in on me.

From there I went to a big hall with about thirty men and thirty bunks back to back. I didn't know a soul. I went in and found my bunk, P9. For the entire time I was locked up in Caldwell, I had to answer to P9. I thought about being in the south with no rights. At least I had my name. Now I'm in the north, locked up with no rights and no name. I went from being called a nigger to being called P9. I would rather be called a nigger than be called P9. I didn't have to answer to nigger. I had to answer to P9.

I checked out the other inmates and got to know one of the guys. He got me a job in the kitchen. I was the server and the pot washer. It was like being back in the hospital. Only I wouldn't see Mrs. Scottsburg's sweet face.

One day one of the inmates wanted two pieces of chicken. I know I wasn't supposed to give them more than one piece so I didn't. I didn't want to ruin anything that would get me out of there when I was supposed to be released. He told me, "I'll take care of you later!"

I thought to myself, "All this for a piece of chicken."

I didn't think anything of it until later that night when I saw a group of guys hunched over together. This was about seven o'clock in the evening. They was waiting for lights out at nine and I knew they was coming for me. From day one, every night I asked, "Lord, please protect me. Whatever you do Lord, protect me." I know mama and everybody else praying for me too. I fell asleep praying, "Lord protect me." I know if He was gonna take care of Martha and the family then He going to take care of me in here too.

Quarter to nine, around seven guards come through the bunk room yelling, "Raid! Raid!" They tore up every bunk in the room. I don't know what they was looking for but they tore up the room! I don't know what they found but what I do know is that same group of guys I saw hunched over was carried out the cell block. When I got my bunk together and lay down I fell asleep saying "Lord I thank you."

Around three o'clock in the morning I felt a draft on me. I turned over in the bunk and looked up toward the window. I saw a white dove at the window flapping his wings. I rubbed my eyes and looked again and it wasn't there. But sometime during the night I heard God as clear as day tell me, "You take care of what's in here and I'll take care of what's out there." In the morning I called Martha and told her, "Baby, the Lord spoke to me last night. I'm not worried no more."

I worked in the kitchen for another week. My brother Big Will brought a work release application in and gave it to the head man. He Okayed it and a week later I started working for Old Deerfield Fabrics as a janitor and groundskeeper. I worked there from six in the morning and had to be back at the jail by five. Big Will picked me up and dropped me off. He was there for me.

I was on work release for about three months. After I served my time, I was free to return to 149 Willowdale Avenue. The morning I was released, Martha and Rivers come to pick me up. I had to stop at the office to get all my belongings. When I got my money, they had short-changed me ten or fifteen dollars. They told me I had to wait for it and I said "Keep it or mail it to me." I didn't want to see another minute of that place. Not for fifteen dollars.

As I was leaving one of the guards looked at me and said, "You'll be back and I'll be here waiting for you." Most of the guys that get released come back. They were repeats. Some of the repeat offenders go out and make trouble just because they don't have nowhere to go. I knew I had somewhere to go and somebody to go to. I had something to do and was gonna finish the good work the Lord placed in me. I didn't want to ruin any chance of me leaving so I held my tongue from what the old Paul might say. But I did say, "If you waiting on me you be without a job."

Old Deerfield Fabric Factory was so good to me that I continued to work with them as I ran my floor waxing business. I kept all my same customers. Imagine that—all my customers waited for me to come back!

Every Wednesday I had to report to my probation officer. I went every week on time and without any problems. One day my probation officer told me "Paul, you wasting my time and yours. You don't have to come here every week. Just call." When I got down to my last three weeks of probation, he called and said I needed to come down.

"How you feeling Paul?"

"I'm doing just fine." I thought I was called down because I was gonna get early parole.

"Can I get a urine sample from you?"

I know I was down to three weeks and I wasn't fool enough to make no mistakes. I was clean and was gonna stay clean. God delivered me from the belly of the whale like Jonah. He appointed a great fish to swallow me up and keep me there for one hundred eighty days and nights. He heard my cry and heard my voice. He cast me deep into the storm and my soul shouted out. I was spit out of the belly of death and now I am free.

CHAPTER TEN
Train up a Child

Train up a child in the way he should go:
and when he is old he will not depart from it
Proverbs 22:6

When I tell you about the things that happen in my life, I'm sharing a part of myself that I hope help you along the way. Maybe you see something in my life that helps you in your walk. The old Paul been swallowed up into the belly of the whale and the new Paul was spit out. When you got nothing else to do but think, you think about all the bad things you done and all the good things you have done. You put them on a scale and weigh them. The good outweighed the bad for me.

Some people have a pail with holes in it. They never seal it up. But once God seal it, don't open it back up again. It was not hard for me to get back on the right foot with God. He brought me from a long way. I was working long hours a day to get back on my feet. It didn't take me long to do that and to get right with the Lord.

Martha was working hard too. She stayed healthy. Everything was going well. I was having a nice time with my family. We were doing a lot of things together. I was still smoking marijuana though. I know that was not good for me. I asked God to take that from me. As soon as I ask God to take it away He took it away. I didn't have to go away to rehab for my habit. I knew if I held on long enough God would restore me. If you going through something you can't handle on your own, give it to God. Just hold on—He knows what you is going through.

One day, Martha ask me, "I haven't seen you smoking cigarettes or pot." I said, "You will never see me smoke cigarettes or marijuana again."

She said, "Well, if God did that for you, he will do the same for me." Martha loved to drink her Smirnoff vodka and cold Rheingold Extra dry beer. She dipped snuff too. It used to bother me that she dipped snuff. But how can I down her for her habit when I got my own? God healed her from all her habits. We were both drug free and it felt good to know there ain't gonna be no more drugs or alcohol in our home. If we was having peoples over, I tell them, "We not drinking no more so I don't want it in the house." Being clean was the best feeling we ever had.

Me and Martha was talking about how good God had been to us. She said, "I don't want to go through that pain again. I will ask God to take me home before I go through that again. She was talking about her brain tumor. Did she know something she wasn't telling me?

A number of years passed. I was at work when my kids called. "Dad I think you should come home"

I came straight home. When I got home and saw Martha's face I knew it wasn't good. Her right eye was swollen and bulging out. It looked like somebody hit her in the face with a baseball. I knew right then something was wrong. I immediately thought back to the first time she got sick with a tumor. I called the hospital and the doctor told me to bring her right in. We got there about 5:30 in the evening. We sat in the waiting room until six the next morning. When they finally took her back into the examination room, me and the kids fell asleep in the waiting room. The doctor and two nurses came out and woke me.

"Your wife is brain dead, Mr. Seaborn."

"What...what you telling me?" Even though I heard them, I thought I might've heard them wrong. This happen before and she was alright. I thought she was gonna be alright again. But I know I heard them right. We been sitting in the waiting room for over twelve hours. I know it wasn't good.

The last thing Martha told the kids was "be good until mama come home." Now I got to tell them there mama won't be coming home. How do you tell a twelve and a fourteen year old child that their mama is dead? I didn't know what to say. I was still in shock. I had to get myself together before I could go to them to tell them anything about their mother.

Before I told them, I called my tenant Rivers. "Martha dead." Rivers didn't believe me. When it sunk in, she almost broke down. She said, "I'm on the way." I told the kids that their mother was dead. They were screaming and hollering. People we didn't know come over to us to try to comfort them. When Rivers got there she was able to calm the children down. The doctor was still talking to me. I had called my Pastor and he came over to talk to the children as well. I had a beautiful relationship with my pastor. There was nothing I couldn't talk to him about. He come Johnny on the spot. He was right beside me the whole time.

This was where my faith really kicked in. Martha was my backbone. She took care of the house, the children and all the bills. Without her I'd be lost. I prayed and asked God for direction.

I buried Martha a week after she died. We had a beautiful home going service at the Vineyard Baptist Church. She was laid to rest in a white casket covered in a white shroud. There were over five hundred people packed into the church, and just as many outside. Me and Martha was well-known in town. She did a lot of things in the community. We buried Martha in Rosedale Cemetery six blocks from the house. The children were still heartbroken. They had a tough time but everybody was good to them. You know, for such a sad time, it really was a beautiful home going. Martha deserved it.

A few months after Martha passed I was looking for some paperwork and what did I find? Martha kept a file cabinet with all of our important papers and bills. All of my household bills were in this file cabinet. I didn't know. I left all this to Martha. I couldn't read so I had to trust that she was taking care of everything. There was a notebook with every bill we had with the price beside it. It was like she know I was gonna need it one day. I know she was looking down on me and our two children. Whenever I be looking for something, I just call Martha's name. "Baby, show me where it's at?" I find it most of the time. It's as if she was watching everything I done.

Thank God for Bernice and my nieces. They showed up for me when I needed them. They showed me how to write out checks. They made a large chart and wrote out every number from one to a thousand. When I was ready to pay my bills, I know how to write the numbers. The world is a better place when you know how to do some things. I relied on Martha for so much. Now I was relying on Bernice and my nieces. I still have that chart to this day. When you put God first there is nothing he won't do. I am a living witness.

Zenas and Paulie took their mama's death real hard. They was having problems in school. I didn't know if it was because of Martha's death. Mama wanted me to give the children to her. I didn't want that. They knew my rules and Martha wouldn't want me to do that. It was my job to raise them. When they got home from school I had to sit them down to have a talk with them. I was having a hard time but I know somebody had to step in. I did what a parent was supposed to do. So I sat down with them and we had a long talk.

"We have to be strong for each other. That's the only way we gonna make it. I want the both of you to think about all the good times we had together with your mama. When you do, you gonna feel real good. She want both of you to finish school and be able to have a good life. I want the same thing for you. When you need someone to talk to, dad is always here."

For the next three years it was just me and my two children. Zenas and Paulie were going to school. I was working hard to take care of them and doing what I had to do. I was not looking for a relationship. I was too busy working and raising my two children. A relationship was the last thing on my mind. I had enough troubles. I was not adding anything else.

After things had been going pretty well for us, one morning Zenas left out the house for school. I happened to stop by the school to check on them. They never know when I'm gonna show up. This was one of those days. The principal took me to Zenas' class. The teacher told me she wasn't in class all day. I got off early and went home to wait for her. When she come in asked her, "How was school today?"

"It was good." I knew she was lying and she knew she was lying.

"Stop lying to me. I went to your school today. Your teacher told me you weren't there all day."

She looked at me funny. I say, "I know you weren't at school today. And what is that on your neck?" She had a big red hickey on her neck. And she gonna tell me a mosquito done bit her!

I took my belt off and started whooping her. I guess I hit her a little too hard because she had a big bruise on her leg. The next morning she went to school acting like her leg was killing her. The teacher sent her to the school nurse. The nurse asked her what happened.

"My daddy whooped me yesterday."

I don't know who did it but somebody at the school called DYFS on me. The New Jersey Division of Youth and Family Services and the Montclair police showed up at my door. They didn't know what was waiting for them.

"Come on in" I say.

"Mr. Seaborn we got a report from your daughter that you whooped her and left a mark on her."

"She lucky she only got a mark on her! When I send her out of here to go to school, that is where I mean for her to go. They is not to go nowhere else. I pay the bills here, put a roof over her head and feed her. She is going to do what I tell her!"

They looked at me but didn't interrupt me.

"I'm a single parent and I'm not gonna go through this with them, not now or later—so please don't tell me how to raise my children!"

"We understand Mr. Seaborn. But if you have to discipline your children, try to do it a little softer. Don't leave marks on their bodies. We'll have to get involved."

"Okay, thank you then—I'm late for work." And I never heard from DYFS again.

And for awhile, everything stayed normal. A few years later when Zenas turned eighteen and was a senior in high school, she got pregnant. It was a few months before she was to graduate.

She tried to hide it from me but I knew. I used to keep a check on tampons and sanitary napkins because I had to buy them. I saw they weren't being used. Then she started walking around the house with her jeans unbuttoned. That's really what made me take notice but I still didn't say anything to her. One day we went to church and sister Lovenia come to me and say, "Deacon, there something I want to talk to you about."

"You don't have to tell me" I say.

"You know what I want to talk to you about?"

"Yes Sister Lovenia. Zenas is pregnant."

"How do you know this Deacon?"

"I'm her daddy. I see how she be going through the house with her jeans all unbuttoned. They were not fitting her right."

"She was afraid to tell you. She knows you don't like her boyfriend."

"Well she don't need to be scared to tell me nothing. What's done is done. She is grown."

Zenas left home after I found out she was pregnant. She moved in with her boyfriend and his mother. He was no good to her. He only wanted her social security check. She and Paulie were getting a few hundred dollars a month from their mother's death.

Then, this boy gonna take her downtown to the police station. He made her tell the police that I raped her. Montclair police showed up at my house again. "Mr. Seaborn, we got to take you in because your daughter is down at the station with her boyfriend accusing you of rape."

Hearing that took everything out of me. Felt like somebody sucker-punched me. I rather that to happen; at least I know what I'm dealing with! Here I was doing everything for my children, doing the best that I could do and she gonna lie on me like that. Even the police didn't believe her. I get to the station, Zenas was there waiting for me.

"Is this what you telling peoples daddy did to you?"

She couldn't even look at me. She was looking at the boyfriend and she was scared. They took him out the room and put me in another room. Then they asked her, "Did your daddy really rape you?"

"No sir" Zenas said. "My boyfriend said he was gonna beat me up if I didn't say that."

The police arrested the boyfriend and locked him up.

I knew when I first saw him that he wasn't the guy for her. He was no good. But it was too late to do anything about it. She was grown now. I took Zenas home and asked her why she did it.

She lowered her head in shame. "I was scared."

That's all she said and that was all I needed to hear.

A few days pass. I get home from work and Zenas not home again. No note, nothing. I told myself if she wasn't home by midnight I wasn't going to look for her. I know she was shacking up with that no good Negro. Everybody knew he was beating on her. Even the boy's mother told Zenas he was no good for her. Peoples would come up to me telling me they saw Zenas and her children in town looking beat down and hungry. I didn't want to hear it. She left on her own and there was nothing I could do. I tell peoples I appreciate what they trying to do but don't tell me if they see her. I knew I had to keep my distance or else I probably kill that boy.

I demanded a certain standard from my children. My mama and daddy expected certain things from their children. I'm thankful for it too. I let my children know where I was coming from. I didn't have no women coming through my house, no liquor or drugs. I wanted them to know that with their mama gone they had to do their part for us to get along. If we can't do right by each other, they need to go.

Almost two years passed. One night I was in bed and I hear a car pull up in my driveway. It was a taxi carrying Zenas and her two children. They run out the taxi and just fall into my arms! Before this the children wouldn't let me touch them. They always see their father beating on their mother and I guess they thought all men do this. But oh my God, they smelled nasty and looked dirty, like they was living on the streets! They was hungry. I fed them. They ate like they hadn't had a meal their whole life.

Zenas left home at eighteen with one child. She came back at twenty with two. What happened to her during those two years is between Zenas and the good Lord. I was glad to have her home. At least I know she has a roof over her head, food in her belly and with someone that love her. She was home. My grandbabies was home. I thank God for delivering her back home.

Zenas say, "Daddy, I'm home. I'm home for good."

Zenas stayed with me for about two years. I gave her what was due her. I gave her forty thousand dollars. That was the inheritance from her mother's hospital settlement. I brought her to Baltimore where she started a new life. She moved in with her cousin until she found a place of her own. She didn't work; she didn't go back to school. She lived on her forty thousand dollars. By the end of the year she was almost broke. She had just enough left to start over in another place. So I packed her up again and moved her to North Carolina. This is where she lives today with her four children. I thank God that today she and my grandchildren is doing just fine. Zenas has worked hard for a number of years. She is now operating her own daycare center. She married a kind young man that she went to high school with. They bought a nice home and are raising a beautiful family. I have four beautiful grandchildren that she gave me: Tamara, Chante, Joseph and Heaven. The two oldest are out on their own. We talk every week.

I call Zenas the angel that God sent me and Martha. Without her there wouldn't have been Adrian. Zenas was a chosen child that actually made a family for me and Martha. I tell her to this day that she is a blessed child. In other words, you don't get to be picked every day. She is like a dozen red roses in a flower garden. A lot of the flowers get picked over until you find the perfect ones. She is the perfect flower we picked out of the garden that day.

There is a saying, "Give a person their flowers while they is living." That is what Zenas did for us. And now I am doing that for her. To this day she is still my baby.

CHAPTER ELEVEN
The Prodigal Son

...for this thy brother was dead,
and is alive again; was lost, and is found.
Luke 15:32

When Paulie was a senior in High School he was one of the best football players on the team. He played for the Cobras of Montclair. A lot of schools were scouting him. He had offers from some of the top schools in the country. They wanted him to play football for them. Paulie wasn't big but he was fast and strong. When he got out there with those guys you would of thought he was bigger than he was because he could drag two or three guys down the line.

I come home and the answering machine be filled with messages from coaches trying to get us to visit their schools. I left it up to Paulie. After he got it down to about five schools, he settled on the University of Maine. I don't know why he picked it but that's who we called. He was offered a five year full scholarship even though his grades weren't where they were supposed to be. He would have to go to special prep classes to help him bring his grades up. He never got that far.

During this time I met my current wife Effie. I had asked God to put another good woman in my life. I knew her cousin Bill. We were good friends. He gave me her number and I called her. We met one Sunday at her house in East Orange. I was sharp as a tack. I wore a pink double-breasted suit and pink shoes. This was the time that men had Jeri curls. I proudly sported one myself! I had gold chains around my neck, big rings and gold bracelets. I was pimped out! And yes, I had pink shades on. I think I had every color sun glasses that was made. I had so many shades that if I threw a birthday party, that's what peoples brought me as a gift.

I thought Effie liked me but she was playing hard to get. Me, Bill and Effie went to Harrison Diner. We talked for hours.

A few months passed before I brought her to the house. I had made a promise to my children that I would never bring any other woman into our house while they was there. God had already showed me that Effie was gonna be my wife. But I had to wait until the children was gone. I didn't want no problems between my woman and my children. If I wait, I don't have to choose between them. Effie wanted to get married. I knew this. I told her if it was meant for us to be together, it was gonna be that way.

We been together for a few months when I told her, "I don't know how to read." I could see she was surprised. Why would she think I couldn't read? I had a couple businesses, dressed nice, and drove nice cars. I wasn't worried about her going nowhere. She was a good Christian woman. She wasn't going to judge me. I know God was gonna send me a good woman. I didn't know when, I didn't know where but I had to hold on to faith. I know God will do it. When my children got out of high school and on their own, I said, "It's time for me to do me now." I wasn't getting no younger.

Me and Effie loaded up my old Cadillac and carried Paulie from Montclair to Maine. We got him to the University of Maine and got him checked in. I talked with the coach and left. I spoke with the coach weekly.

Everybody at school knew Paulie by Adrian. That was the name on his birth certificate. All of the family called him Paulie. The coach said Adrian wasn't doing what he was supposed to do for his grades so he gave him a curfew. Paulie was into the girls and not hitting the books as he should. The coach talked to me and told me where Paulie stood. I called Paulie and said, "Look, you is there for one reason…to get a college education. Do what you got to do and get out!"

His first game of the season he got hit and injured his leg. From there he was never right. He went wild. He was in school for a year when the coach called and says, "I'm sorry Mr. Seaborn but Adrian is kicked out of school. You have to come pick him up." Hearing those words hit me harder than when I got sentenced. This was his future. He had a good life right in front of him and he was blind to it. I made a way for him. I laid everything out for him. I didn't have that opportunity. Nobody paid my way for nothing. What I have I had to work hard for. If I had the opportunities he had, I would be reading and writing long ago. But instead, here I stand, a man who can't read or write. I had earned and saved enough money for him to go to college. He didn't have to use my money. He was given an opportunity to go to college on the man. And he blew it. I was broken. It didn't feel good but I know I had to bring him home.

About a year and a half later he said he wanted to go back to school. He come to me and ask if I can pay for it. "You blow a one hundred twenty five thousand dollar scholarship and you gave it back to the state because you don't know how to do right?"

I was hot by under the cuff by now. He know I saved money for his education. "Now don't think that money is yours", I tell him. I had a feeling he was going to try to ask for it. I was too mad to even think straight. But that wasn't the end of the story.

Before we took Paulie to Maine, I put forty thousand dollars in an account for him. The same forty I gave Zenas.

This is how I come across that money. I got a settlement from a wrongful death lawsuit I brought against the hospital. I been trying to find an attorney who would take the case. One day I was waxing a client's office floors when I told him my story. He been a customer of mine for many years. He had a huge law practice with about twenty five lawyers under him.

"I'll take it on" he said. "If we win you pay me, if we don't, it's on me."

The suit went on for three years before the hospital finally came in with a settlement offer. My attorney turned it down. Three or four months later the hospital come back with another offer. This time we took it. It was enough for me to pay the attorney and each child to get forty thousand dollars apiece and I got the rest. I asked him, "Do my children have to get this money? I know what they gonna do with it."

"When they turn eighteen it's theirs."

There was nothing I could do about it. I sat them down and told them where this money come from. I expected them to use that money wisely. They both went through it before the year was over. I was hoping they be smarter with it. It was theirs to do with as they please. I can't tell them how to spend it just like they can't tell me how to spend my money.

A few years later I went to Baltimore to visit mama and daddy. Effie's niece told me about some townhomes that were for sale. I went to talk with him. He told me, "You can have them for three hundred fifty thousand dollars."

I knew he was asking too much. I offered him what I thought they was worth. He turned it down. Another two weeks passed when he called again. He asked me, "When can we meet?"

I drove down the next week and we closed the deal. I couldn't find a bank at the time that would give me a mortgage. I went to my attorney. I put one hundred thousand dollars down and took money out of some other properties I had. The owner of the townhouses held the mortgage for about a year. I was now owner of fourteen townhouses. We put in everything new; sinks, carpets, paint, vanities, everything. They were nice when we finished fixing them up. I hired a management company to take care of them. I was still living in Montclair at the time. The management company was taking money and not doing the work. The tenants tell me nothing was being done. So I got rid of them and moved to Baltimore to take care of my own properties.

When I get to Baltimore, I was busy. Maryland General Hospital was adding a large section of rooms and needed someone to do the floors. Minnie Mae was working in housekeeping. She told her boss about me and they called. I took the job. I hired some help and completed it as promised. When I finished the job, they asked me if I want to work for the hospital. So I took the job working sixteen hours a day, seven days a week. I maintained my townhouses with the help of my friend Butch. It wasn't easy. I asked God for direction. He guide me through that time.

About three years passed. It was getting harder and harder to keep up my relationship with Effie. I called Effie and ask her, "Would you be willing to give up your job and move to Baltimore?" She been there for twenty something years.

She answered, "I have to think about it." I know that was asking her a whole lot. She thought about it and called me. "Yes" she said.

I know Effie was meant for me. She come to Baltimore about a year later. When she got there we looked for apartments. We found a one bedroom apartment. I went to New Jersey and moved her to Baltimore in my 1970 Cadillac. Peoples was looking at me with all this furniture piled on top of my car. I guess they was wondering where we was going looking like the Beverly Hillbillies. I stopped buying new cars all the time. Matter of fact, I kept the same car for a good while.

Three years later I asked Effie to marry me. I asked my Pastor Carter if I could make an announcement. I proposed to her in church in front of the whole congregation after service. She said "Yes!" We got married the same year. We had over three hundred people at the wedding and reception.

Up until two months before Effie and me got married, I didn't see Paulie for six years. I was working one day and there was a message on my answering machine. "Paulie is heading home", the voice said. I called my mother and she said, "Guess who is here?"

"Paulie" I say.

"Well son, how you know it was Paulie?"

"Because a woman left a message saying he was on his way home." To this day I never knew who left that message on my answering machine.

For about six years I didn't know where my son was. One Sunday in church, Pastor asked us to write a letter to God. "Whatever you want God to do put it in the letter." I still didn't know how to read but I could write a little. I couldn't write a letter but I knew how to spell Paulie's name. I put his name in the four corners and folded it up. Only two people knew what that meant— God and me. Even if I couldn't write his name and only folded up the piece of paper, God would know what I meant. I put the paper in an addressed envelope, sealed it, put a stamp on it and placed it in the basket. The next week at church, the letter come back to me. Pastor handed the letters back to everyone. Two weeks after that I brought my son to church. God answered my prayer and brought my son home. I stood up and gave my testimony.

"Remember three weeks ago when Pastor asked us to write a letter. I wanted my son to be at my wedding. I put my son's name on each corner of the paper and sealed it. When pastor give the letter back to me last week I know my prayer was answered. A week later my son showed up at my mama's house. Today my son is here with me."

I called out to him by the name me and Martha gave him at birth. I said "Adrian—Stand up!"

I was up at the altar. I didn't know if he would lift off the pew and come down the aisle to me or not. But I do know that whatever the good Lord had done, He done it for me. I remembered a verse from Ephesians, "For by grace I had been saved through faith; and that not of myself, but it is the gift of God." This was my gift from God.

Paulie walked down the aisle to me. The deacons and ushers and pastors prayed over us. That was a good feeling that day.

Paulie come home with only the clothes on his back. What he was doing all those years we never talked about. I know he got mixed up in drugs. I know he ran around. But who is I to cast a stone. He didn't do nothing that I didn't do. He drove a car home with no driver's license. I made him hand over the keys.

He stayed with mama and daddy until I found him a place. Me and Effie paid his rent for three months. We took him shopping for new clothes. I took him everywhere helping him find a job. I told him, "As long as you do right, daddy is here for you." Paulie looked me straight in the eyes and said, "Daddy, I'm ready to change." He got a security job at a hospital fourteen years ago. He is still there today.

I know a change was gonna come. I asked God to deliver my son and He did. I never doubted that. When I put Paulie's name on the four corners of that wrinkled paper, I knew my prayer was already answered.

Soon after that I saw my son and he come up to me and hugged me real hard. He said, "Daddy, I'm sorry." He cried like a baby. He was broken.

In other words, Paulie had to go to the mourners' bench too. We all got to get down on our hands and knees and ask the Lord for forgiveness for something. We got to let go of the troubles that weigh us down—that hold us back. We got to know that even after the darkest night, in the morning everything gonna be alright. We can bring it all to the Lord in prayer.

Paulie always wanted to be like me. I always wanted to be like my daddy. But Paulie, he had his mother's ways. He had my instincts but Martha's ways. He wasn't a dresser. He didn't like to hang in the bars. He wasn't the party type. I owned a night club. No, Paulie like to fish and work with his hands. He is a smart man. He's got his mother's wit.

Now Paulie is grown with his own family. He has two beautiful children; Mariah and Adriana. The day that Paulie was born, I knew that God had answered prayers for me and Martha. God gave us a girl named Zenas and now I have a son. I trained him up the way he should go. Maybe my example wasn't always right but I did my best. I tried to keep the worse of me away from my children. Paulie is my only son and I love him to death. He might have gone astray but he found his way back. God showed him the way home.

I thought about the prodigal son. He run off with everything. When he lost everything and had nothing else, he come back. His father took him in. I knew that's what I had to do. Forget about old mess and start new.

CHAPTER TWELVE
Let Not Your Heart Be Troubled

...Lord, we know not whither thou goest;
and how can we know the way?
Jesus saith unto him,
I am the way, the truth, and the life:
no man cometh unto the Father, but by me.
John 14:5, 6

Three years before Effie and I got married, we started going to Little Ark Missionary Baptist Church. Every Sunday morning at 9:30 we go to Sunday school. I always liked Sunday school because it felt like I was in school learning. I still couldn't read or write but nobody except Effie knew that. Didn't matter though, I could listen and get something out of what was being said. I loved hearing the different stories and verses. I enjoyed hearing everybody talk about the bible.

I was a faithful member at church. Pastor asked me to be a walking Deacon. That mean I do things that others ask me to do. It was like being on probation. I was like an assistant deacon. All the deacons watch me do my duties around the church. They also observe how I carry myself and care for others in and out of the church. I did all the duties of a deacon except for anything that had to do with reading. That I made sure of.

Sister Wilson was teaching Sunday school one morning when she said, "Brother Aron, please read the first nine verses of this morning's focal verses." I don't know if she knew I couldn't read but right then and there I knew I had to make a confession. I was tired of living a lie. Besides, I'm sitting in God's house, how can I tell a lie?

I could not read what I was looking at. Every Sunday morning I be looking in my Sunday school book, pretending to follow along with everyone else. I was found out! I felt like a little kid that sneaked something he wasn't supposed to have.

All these years I wasn't expected to be successful in business. I wasn't supposed to have a beautiful wife and children. I wasn't supposed to have custom made suits and gold jewelry hanging from my neck. I shouldn't have cars and homes. No, if you can't read or write, what you supposed to have? What you supposed to be? Nothing. I always wanted to be more than nothing. So I made it not knowing how to read or write. I was doing better than most people's I knew that could read and write. I got my education. I learned the hard way—on the farms and on the streets!

I didn't need books. And I could do a lot of things a whole lot smarter than them who went to school.

But still, I was found out. There was no place I could turn—no place I could run and hide. No, it was time for me to fess up to something that was weighing me down for years. I had to put pride aside. I had to humble myself before the Lord. I don't know why she picked me that hot Sunday morning. It was not for me to question. I had to admit to my secret. I had to tell the truth. The Lord was watching me now, waiting to see what I was gonna say and do. He brought me this far. I couldn't let Him down again.

"Sister Wilson, I'm sorry but I don't know how to read."

I could have been from another planet with the way everybody turned and looked at me. And even though I was on the spot, I wasn't embarrassed. I felt like the weight of the world had lifted off of me. Once I heard those words, "I can't read" come out of my mouth, I felt like a new person. I felt like I was kneeling at the mourner's bench, asking for God to forgive me my sins. This time, I meant it. I felt like I was born again, like God was opening a new door for me. I now know this door was always open, the good Lord was waiting for me to walk through it. He puts peoples on our paths that lead to the open door.

This time He used Sister Wilson. I considered Sister Wilson my guardian angel that opened the doorway to heaven. I wasn't ashamed or afraid anymore. This was the first time that I publicly come out to say that I didn't know how to read. I said it in front of room full of peoples. Before now, it been to my first wife and then to Effie. People might have known, but it wasn't because I told them.

After Sunday school, Sister Wilson pointed her finger at me and told me, "Come here Paul!" I walked up front to her with my head held high it seemed like for the first time.

"Monday morning, I want you at my house at 9:00. I'm going to teach you how to read the bible."

That same Sunday, talk had started spreading, "How Pastor gonna make him a deacon and he can't even read?" Hearing that in the past would have bothered me. Now, what was in me was out of me. God had sent help for me. How could I feel bad about that? Sister Wilson told me, "Don't let anybody discourage you about what you told us. You are just as important as they are. It don't matter anymore that you can't read. I'm going to teach you."

Pastor Carter understood too. He later ordained me as a deacon. He said, "The person doing all the talking about you isn't doing anything in and for the church—and he can read!" That's how people be. Even in the church some peoples are against you. But everybody got to go to their own mourners' bench and get it right before God. My knees are worn but my spirit is finally free!

I met with Sister Wilson five days a week for over a year. Sister Wilson was a spicy little lady for her age. She was a short, thin woman that always wore colorful African clothes. She kept her braided hair under a turban. She was a story teller, a griot. She travelled everywhere telling stories. They called her Tunku. Every morning we read and she would encourage me to keep going. When we finish reading she explain to me what we read. Then she ask me what I took from the lesson. She was testing my comprehension.

After about year Sister Wilson took sick and couldn't teach me no more. I visit her in the nursing home every day. We always read the bible. I bring her food and anything else she asked for. Soon it was hard to see her lose life because before she took ill she was so lively. She was so good to me. If it hadn't been for Sister Wilson I probably wouldn't be in school today.

Before she died she told her daughters that she wants me to read from John 14 at her funeral. If I knew the verse I maybe could have gone and practiced it. But I was too emotional to try to read. I maybe would have stuttered and dragged out each word for too long. I didn't want to mess up nothing. I was only just learning how to read. I probably wasn't reading more than a first grader. Like I said, if I learned the verses I could have said it from memory but I didn't want to do that. It would have felt like the same lie I was delivered from when I confessed. So I had to ask Effie to read it for me. I said the prayer. I could do that because there was so much in my heart I wanted to say. I loved Sister Wilson. There is not a day go by that I don't think about her. When I finished the prayer, Effie read from the King James Bible, the book of John, chapter 14.

"Do not let your hearts be troubled. You believe in God, believe also in me. My Father's house has many rooms; if that were not so, would I have told you that I am going to prepare a place for you? And if I go and prepare a place for you, I will come back and take you to be with me that you also may be where I am. You know the way to the place where I am going..."

Epilogue

Through my struggle I know there is someone else out there going through the same thing. They is afraid to come forward. I plead for them to get the weight off of them. They been carrying it around for so many years. Know that help is on the way. You just have to open up. I am a living witness to what God will do in your life. Regardless of what anyone say, I wouldn't be where I am today if I had listened to what peoples said about me. I was freed, knowing that God was the only one that gave me victory.

I feel like somebody that never had the opportunity to walk in their life and now I am able to walk on my own. Now I can tell you how I feel, knowing that now I can read and write. Even now, at the age of seventy two, I am able to read and write this book with help. I knows how to write out checks and pay my own bills. That is a good feeling. That is what God will do. Just be obedient.

I feel better about my life. Now I have the opportunity to go to school four days a week. I am learning what I didn't learn as a child. They took away the books but they didn't take away my mind. I been given a chance to learn. Learning is something that I really enjoy doing. School is my life right now. I won't quit until God says so.

Life is like a pail with holes in it. But when you pray and ask God to change your life, all holes are filled. Now everything you put in the pail stays in. God has sealed all holes, all old wounds, and made you brand new again. I was that pail. When God saw me, lying beside the road, he saw a pail with holes in it. God took that pail, molded it, shaped it, gave me arms and legs, gave me heart, and he plugged up the holes. Then he breathed into my nostrils and said, "This is the new Paul, arise and walk!" That's where the old Paul has died and the new Paul is on the scene.

As of this writing, I am at a fifth grade reading level. I can read the newspaper, the bible, magazines and books. I don't understand all the words. I don't always understand what I am reading. The newspaper be the hardest for me to read right now. But I get the paper every morning and sit at the kitchen table and read through it over a cup of hot coffee. I can read enough most time to understand what is happening. I read my bible every day too. I can follow along in Sunday school without pointing to every word on the page. When the Pastor say turn to a chapter, I knows where to go.

Every Thursday, I meet with my tutor Carol Williams at the Lancaster County Library. She saw something in me and I thank her. She takes time out of her day each week to help me on my journey. Some days I go to the library and check out books. I had a lot of books at home before I could even read. I've read Gifted Hands by Ben Carson. I've read it more than once. I guess I can relate to a lot of the ways he grew up. I also read the Martin Luther King story. Books mean a lot to me now. I didn't know anything about black history besides what I lived through. Now I can read about it. I can do my own research. I did my own research on Frederick Douglas. My teachers at Lancaster Adult Learning helped me too. They helped me read. They helped me talk different than I used to. I still have a long way to go, but I am pressing on.

I find myself saying words that I never said before. I was used to speaking a certain way so that is how I write. Now I try to speak the right way. It is hard to break an old habit but I am working on it. Throughout this book, you read it as I say it or think it. I don't always use contractions. I am just learning about them. When I first started reading I run into those words and I wondered "well where the other part of the word at?" Now I know the apostrophe takes the place of that word. But it is still something I has to get used to. It is something I have to go through as I learn. Sometimes I put an S where it don't go. Sometimes I take it off where it belong. I don't do well with past tense. I guess you figure that out by now. That is how I talk so for now, this is how I write. I will keep learning until I gets it right!

All that I have gone through, if I had to do it over again, there is one thing in my life I would change. That would be my involvement with drugs. I can't really explain how I feel about it but I would ask God to take that part of my life away. I'll take the hard life, the lessons; the not being able to read. I can't ask for any better life than I have. God has looked out for me through it all. He has delivered a sinner like me. I can't ask for no more.

Special Appearances

Would you like to hear Aron "Paul" Seaborn share his fascinating story with your company or organization? His poignant delivery is engaging, inspiring and one of the most heart-rending, motivating speeches you will ever hear. Secure him now!

Please contact:
Melanie Calloway
M. Patrice Group LLC
www.mpatricegroup.com
704-280-8322 office

Look for Aron Seaborn on Facebook, Twitter, YouTube and Instagram. Stay up-to-date on appearances, special offers, and more! Be sure to share, like and retweet!

A portion of all Aron Seaborn book sales and appearances is
donated to the
Aron and Effie Seaborn Literacy Initiative.
To find out how you can help, please visit AESLI.org

On behalf of the author, publisher and its management we thank you
for your support.